T0361042

Doing Economics

Doing Economics offers a clear and accessible guide to the nature of economics. Unlike many other mainstream disciplines, economics is a subject that many students meet for the first time when they arrive at university to study the subject at degree level. The way economics is studied at university level can vary greatly from economics as represented in the media, but this handy beginner's guide bridges that gap.

This book answers such questions as:

- What is economics as a subject?
- What sorts of questions does it address?
- What skills are needed to become a good economist?
- Where will it take me?

Students will be introduced to the key characters who contributed to the development of economics, as well as to the central ideas and concepts. This definitive guide outlines the attributes that make a good economist and presents a wide variety of employment opportunities that can follow the study of economics. Familiarising students with the important terms and issues, it is an essential volume for all students approaching this fascinating subject.

Peter Smith is Emeritus Professor in Economics at the University of Southampton, UK. He has published textbooks for A-level Economics and produced interactive learning materials to accompany a best-selling first year undergraduate text. He is an Associate of the Economics Network, a Principal Fellow of the Higher Education Academy and a Reviewer for the Quality Assurance Agency.

Also available from Routledge

Economics: The Basics (3rd edition)
Tony Cleaver
978-1-138-02354-3

Finance: The Basics (3rd edition)
Erik Banks
978-1-138-91978-5

Economics: The Key Concepts
Donald Rutherford
978-0-415-40057-2

Routledge Dictionary of Economics (3rd edition)
Donald Rutherford
978-0-415-60038-5

Doing Economics

Peter Smith

Routledge
Taylor & Francis Group

LONDON AND NEW YORK

First published 2016
by Routledge
2 Park Square, Milton Park, Abingdon, Oxon OX14 4RN

and by Routledge
711 Third Avenue, New York, NY 10017

Routledge is an imprint of the Taylor & Francis Group, an informa business

British Library Cataloguing in Publication Data
A catalogue record for this book is available from the British Library

Library of Congress Cataloging in Publication Data
Names: Smith, Peter, 1947– author.
Title: Doing economics / Peter Smith.
Description: 1 Edition. | New York : Routledge, 2016.
Identifiers: LCCN 2015041469 | ISBN 9781138791664 (hardback) | ISBN 9781138791671 (pbk.) | ISBN 9781315762678 (ebook)
Subjects: LCSH: Economics—Textbooks.
Classification: LCC HB171.5 .S6417 2016 | DDC 330—dc23LC
record available at http://lccn.loc.gov/2015041469

ISBN: 978-1-138-79166-4 (hbk)
ISBN: 978-1-138-79167-1 (pbk)
ISBN: 978-1-315-76267-8 (ebk)

Typeset in Bembo
by RefineCatch Limited, Bungay, Suffolk

Contents

List of figures

About the author

Peter Smith is Emeritus Professor in Economics at the University of Southampton. He has taught economics at the University of Southampton for more years than he cares to mention, including teaching at all levels of the undergraduate and postgraduate level. He has supervised more than 20 students to successful PhDs. His specialist area for teaching and research is development economics, and he has also written on economics education. He is Editor of and writes regularly for *Economic Review*, a magazine that is intended for students meeting economics for the first time, which has been published since 1983. He is an Associate of the *Economics Network*, has contributed to their *Handbook for Economics Lecturers*, led workshops on aspects of education in economics and presented papers at the Network's biennial conference on *Developments in Economics Education*. He has written textbooks for AS- and A-level Economics, and is responsible for producing interactive learning exercises to accompany first-year undergraduate textbooks. He is a Reviewer for the Quality Assurance Agency.

Acknowledgements

My own fascination with economics began when I chose it as a subject for A-level because the school timetable did not allow me to take the combination of subjects that I really wanted to study. As an undergraduate at the University of Warwick, my interest grew, and this continued through my time as a researcher at University College London and my years as an academic at the University of Southampton. During that time, many academic colleagues and students have influenced me and indirectly contributed to this volume, which tries to capture some of my enthusiasm for the subject whilst also providing practical advice and guidance for those contemplating the study of economics. I cannot mention all by name, but in particular I would like to thank Helen Paul, who helped me to compile the list of questions to ask at an open (visit) day, and members of the Economics Network, especially those who attended the *Developments in Economics Education* Conference in 2015, which took place when I was in the midst of writing the book.

I would also like to thank the team at Taylor & Francis, in particular Andy Humphries, who approached me with the idea of the book, and Laura Johnson and Alaina Christensen, who guided me in preparing the final version.

Above all, I would like to offer an enormous thank you to my wife Maureen, who not only put up with my obsession with finishing the book, but also read every chapter and made many invaluable suggestions for improvement.

Introduction

This book is intended for those who are considering economics as their subject at university, whether or not they have already taken it at AS- or A-level, or as part of another qualification. It will also be helpful for those who are just beginning their economics degrees.

The time that you spend studying at university can be life-changing. It will strongly influence the course that your career takes, and provides unrivalled opportunities for building a network of friends, some of whom you will know for ever. It can be an exciting time that can shape your personality for the future.

I find it daunting indeed to sit at my computer preparing advice and guidance that can have such an impact!

I chose to study economics at university because I had found it interesting at A-level, and thought I could succeed at it. I was fortunate enough to be among the first students to attend the University of Warwick, and although the campus was a building site, the experience was fantastic, and I was captivated by economics as a subject – and I still am. I hope that some of this enthusiasm for economics will rub off on you, the readers of this book.

This book is not intended to be a textbook, so it does not go into detail about the content of the subject, although it does try to introduce some key ideas to give you a flavour of what it will be like to study economics at university. However, it makes no claim to be a comprehensive introduction to the subject, and I have cherry-picked what I hope will help you to come to a good decision about whether economics is for you. Key technical economics terms appear in **bold** in the text, and are defined in the Glossary on page 141.

The books aims to help you to make good decisions about your choice of programme, but does not attempt to guide you towards a particular university of type of institution, The choice is yours.

It aims to be a practical guide, highlighting important things that you need to know when you are considering setting out on an undergraduate programme in economics.

I hope you find it useful, and that it will encourage you to consider studying economics in the future.

An afterthought before we proceed: on programmes, modules and courses

Economists like to be precise in their use of words, and, at the outset, I would like to comment on an important piece of jargon to avoid possible confusion.

This relates to the word 'programme'. I will use this throughout the book to refer to the whole period of study that you follow at a university, normally lasting three years.

A programme is made up of a number of individual components, which I will refer to as 'modules'. These modules will come together to from the 'programme'.

Except where quoting another author or organisation, I will avoid using the word 'course'. When you visit university websites, you will find that some use 'course' when referring to what I am calling a 'programme', whereas others use 'course' to mean what I will call a 'module'.

PART I

Defining economics

What is economics?

1

This chapter will:

- outline the subject matter of economics
- set out three key questions that lie at the heart of economic analysis
- introduce the main economic agents taking economic decisions
- identify the way that economists approach decision-making and problem-solving
- note the importance of coordinating resource allocation and the potential for economic policy to influence economic decisions and the performance of an economy

Many students meet economics as a subject for the first time when they arrive to study it at university, sometimes with only a vague idea about what it is.

This is partly because economics is not one of those subjects that forms part of the school curriculum from its early years. Almost from day one, pupils begin to learn the three Rs, reading, writing and 'rithmetic. These then evolve into English literature and language and mathematics. Geography, history and the core sciences follow soon after – but not economics.

Economics as a discipline for study thus waits for the last couple of years of school or college, or for university. By the time you start to study economics, you will already have been taking economic decisions and facing economic problems without knowing that you have been doing so. By studying economics as a discipline, you will find that you become more aware of these decisions and problems, and will be able to tackle these more effectively.

A definition of economics?

Defining economics as a discipline is not as easy as you might expect. Perhaps you think that economics is the 'study of the economy', and to some extent that is correct. However, this is too simple, and leaves too many questions unanswered – for a start, this definition would not make sense unless it is absolutely clear what is meant by 'the economy'.

If you were to undertake a Google search on 'economics definition', you would be confronted by a range of possible options. Here are a few examples:

the branch of knowledge concerned with the production, consumption, and transfer of wealth
(The Oxford Dictionary of English as cited by Google)

a science concerned with the process or system by which goods and services are produced, sold, and bought
http://www.merriam-webster.com/dictionary/economics

the study of how people choose to use resources'
The American Economic Association (AEA) at
https://www.aeaweb.org/students/WhatIsEconomics.php

the science which studies human behaviour as a relationship between ends and scarce means which have alternative uses.'
Lionel Robbins (1932, p. 15)

A social science that studies how individuals, governments, firms and nations make choices on allocating scarce resources to satisfy their unlimited wants.
Investopedia at
http://www.investopedia.com/terms/e/economics.asp

Notice that many of these definitions focus more on the processes that economists study, rather than setting out the scope, or the subject matter, of the discipline. Many popular books written by economists in recent years (e.g. Levitt and Dubner and Harford) have expanded horizons by showing how economic thinking can be used to answer any number of questions about aspects of life not normally associated with economics. These offer an entertaining introduction to how economists may think – but do not necessarily provide a foretaste of what it will be like to study the subject at university. Indeed, the Korean economist Ha-Joon Chang of the University of Cambridge has noted that there are many economists who tend to 'define their subject in terms of its theoretical approach, rather than its subject matter' (Chang, 2014).

Introductory textbooks have also tended to shy away from providing a simple definition of the subject. Indeed, many of them also focus on the 'central economic problem' – the problem of coordinating production decisions with consumption. We will explore this more carefully soon.

If you study economics at a UK university, you will find that the programme of study is designed to meet the subject benchmark that is set by the Quality Assurance Agency (QAA), which is the regulator for universities in the UK. In July 2015, the QAA published its latest national subject benchmark for economics, setting out what every undergraduate economics programme in the country is expected to deliver. It therefore makes sense to begin with their statement of what economics is:

> Economics is the study of the factors that influence income, wealth and well-being. From this it seeks to inform the design and implementation of economic policy. Its aim is to analyse and understand the allocation, distribution and utilisation of resources and the consequences for economic and social well-being. Economics is concerned with such phenomena in the past and present and how they may evolve in the future.
>
> http://www.qaa.ac.uk/en/Publications/Documents/
> SBS-Economics-15.pdf, p. 5

This statement sets out what you can expect from a university education in economics. It was produced by a review group composed of academic economists from a range of UK universities together with employer and student representatives. All economics programmes in the UK are required to fulfil the expectations set out in the benchmark statement – which goes on to provide much more detail about the content of programmes and the skills and attributes of an economics graduate. As this book progresses, it will touch base with this document from time to time to explain how it will influence the education that you will receive.

From the quotation, you can begin to appreciate the scope of economic analysis. It is not just about 'money' or the economic indicators that receive attention in the media, such as unemployment or inflation. Economics is about well-being, it is about inequality and it is about the design of economic policy to influence economic aspects of the society in which we live. It is about how society has developed in the past, how it is performing in the present, and how it is likely to develop in the future.

Three questions

The teaching of economics in universities in the period after the Second World War was strongly influenced by Paul Samuelson's *Economics* textbook published in 1948. The nineteenth edition (produced in conjunction with William

Nordhaus) was published in 2009, and the book has influenced generations of economists. Samuelson argued that economics was about three key questions affecting society: *what* is produced, *how* it is produced and *for whom* it is produced.

What is produced?

The resources available to a society are used to produce goods and services. A key question to be analysed is how decisions are taken on what combination of goods and services should be produced to add to the well-being of members of society. For example, how does a society decide how resources should be allocated between goods and services for consumption in the present, as opposed to using resources now that will deliver more goods and services in the future?

How are goods and services produced?

Decisions are also needed concerning how goods and services are produced, given that there are different ways in which this can be accomplished. For example, there may be alternative ways of manufacturing goods making use of workers or automated processes.

For whom are goods and services produced?

The question here is who gets to consume the goods and services that are produced. In other words, how are resources distributed amongst the members of society?

These questions offer what is perhaps a more focused view of the scope of economic analysis than some of the more simple definitions listed earlier, although the questions can be related back to those attempts at defining economics. Let's look at some of the fundamental economic issues that underpin the study of these three questions and introduce some concepts and ideas that you will no doubt encounter early in any study of the discipline.

Economic agents

The definition of economics offered by Investopedia above refers to choices made by 'individuals, governments, firms and nations'. These are the key **economic agents** whose decisions are analysed by economists. It is helpful at this point to say a little about each of them.

Individuals (households)

Households or individuals make two important kinds of economic decisions. As consumers, they take decisions about which goods and services to buy, and in what quantities. Consumer theory is an important part of economic analysis that explores how these decisions are taken. However, people also provide labour, and thus contribute to the production of goods and services, in return earning income that can then be used to buy goods and services.

Governments (nations)

It should be clear that governments also take important economic decisions. Governments impose taxes and undertake expenditure, spending on goods and services and ensuring that the economy works effectively. Governments take those decisions on behalf of the population; in a democratic society, elections provide the mandate for government to take decisions and implement economic policy.

The extent to which governments intervene in the operation of society varies between countries, and the way in which resources are allocated differs – for example, resources are allocated very differently in a democracy such as the UK or the USA than in socialist countries like North Korea or China. This will be explored later in the book.

Firms

Firms are responsible for organising the production of goods and services, and play a crucial role in the economy. As part of this process, they hire labour from households and take important decisions about current and future production.

Scarcity and choice

Early in the chapter, it was claimed that by the time you begin to study economics, you will already have been taking economic decisions and facing economic problems. Let's look more closely at this notion.

It's Saturday morning. You lie in bed for a bit, thinking about how you could spend your day. You could hang out with your friends in the shopping mall or ice cream parlour, or see a new film showing at the cinema. Your local football team has a home match. Or you could spend time making cupcakes because you enjoy baking. You have homework to be done. After some deliberation and a further doze, you text your friends and arrange to meet up in the shopping mall later on.

Why is this an economic decision?

First and foremost, it is because you cannot do everything. There are only so many hours in the day, so you must make a choice. In short, you face a situation of **scarcity**. In this case, the scarcity is forced because of limited time, but it may also reflect your other resources. Perhaps you don't have enough cash to pay for a ticket for the football, or to buy the ingredients to make cupcakes.

For the society as a whole, scarcity is similarly an issue. A society cannot provide all the goods and services that all of its members would like. The underlying issue is that people have unlimited wants, but society faces scarce resources relative to those unlimited wants. The definitions of economics quoted earlier from Robbins and Investopedia both make explicit reference to scarcity as part of their statements.

Scarcity forces choices to be made, and leads to one of the most fundamental of economic concepts.

Opportunity cost

As soon as you choose to take a particular action, you exclude the possibility of some alternative. If you choose to meet up with your friends in the shopping mall, you also choose *not* to do your homework or make cupcakes. This is the cost of your choice, known by economists as the **opportunity cost**. In other words, the opportunity cost is the value of the next best alternative choice that you could have taken, but which must be forgone in favour of your actual choice.

Each of the types of economic agent faces opportunity cost when they take economic decisions. Consumers face an opportunity cost because by choosing to buy a particular good or service, they forgo the possibility of purchasing some other good. When households choose to supply their labour by taking a job, they forgo the leisure time that they could have enjoyed otherwise. When a firm chooses to produce a particular good or service, it forgoes the production of some other good or service. If a government chooses to put more of its resources into the National Health Service, or into defence, it must cut back in some other area of activity, such as education. Opportunity cost is thus an important aspect of all economic decision-making.

In many ways, the interesting question is why an economic agent should choose one alternative over the next best one. Why does a consumer choose to buy one good and forgo another? Why does a firm choose to produce one good rather than another? How does the government choose how to allocate funds between defence and education?

Rational choice?

Much of traditional economic analysis is based on an assumption that economic agents act rationally. Indeed, if we do not have some notion of what firms, individuals and governments are trying to achieve, we cannot hope to understand how they take decisions.

For consumers, the normal assumption is that they set out to gain as much satisfaction from their actions as they can. They will choose one alternative over another because it gives them more satisfaction. To use the economist's jargon, consumers aim to maximise their **utility**, this being the word that economists use to capture the notion of satisfaction. In the example we saw earlier, if an individual chooses to meet up with friends in the shopping mall rather than doing homework or making cupcakes, this is because this is the action that provides most satisfaction at the time. If a person chooses to work an hour's overtime instead of having an additional hour of leisure, that is because the additional earnings from the hour of overtime more than compensate for the hour of leisure.

For firms, it has often been assumed that a firm acts to make as much **profit** as possible. For example, a firm may choose to produce a particular good rather than another because it expects to get a better return from doing so. It aims to *maximise its profit*.

This sort of argument is likely to be an early part of your study of economics at university, but you will also find that as your programme of study progresses, the assumption that economic agents always act rationally will come under close scrutiny, and there is an increasing amount of economists' research time being devoted to this topic, in particular through conducting experiments. We will return to this later in the book.

Decisions at the margin

An important aspect of the economist's approach to analysing decisions is that it is often assumed that economic agents taking decisions may do so by considering small changes to their current position. For example, a firm considering whether to expand its output of a good may think about whether the extra benefit from producing an additional unit of production will exceed the cost of producing it. A consumer may consider whether consuming an additional unit of a good will add more to satisfaction than its cost. Suppose you have just consumed a great meal: would having seconds of dessert make you feel even better? Or will it make you feel ill? Was that fifth ice cream a cornet too far?

As your study of economics progresses, you will realise that this notion of **marginal analysis** is really important if we want to analyse the conditions under which an economic agent can reach the point at which maximisation takes place, whether this be maximising utility, profit or anything else.

Assumptions and models

You will gather from the discussion so far that economic analysis seems to rely heavily on making *assumptions*. This is indeed the case, and one of the most frequent criticisms of economists is that they live in an abstract world that seems remote from the one in which we live, a world that is based on a host of unrealistic assumptions.

This reflects the fact that economics sets out to explain the behaviour of individuals, firms and governments within a highly complex environment.

The 'real' world out there is a complicated place, with millions of people consuming a huge variety of different goods and services that are produced by a multitude of firms that need to decide what goods and services to produce, and to select techniques of production. This all happens within the framework set by a government with objectives of its own, that imposes taxes and makes transfers between groups in society. Without simplifying this complex reality it is impossible to make progress in seeking to explain how it all works.

In order to overcome this, economists build simplifying *models* of reality, based on clear simplifying assumptions. For example, we may build a model that tries to explain why consumers act in the way that they do, based on assumptions such as the one already mentioned – that they set out to maximise their utility.

If it turns out that the world does not work out in the way that a model predicts, we can go back to see if one of the assumptions fails to hold true, or if the logic applied in building the model is false. We can also vary the assumptions to see whether the findings of the model change significantly. By understanding a simplified model, we can begin to learn about how the 'real' world works.

In considering whether economics is for you, it is worth noting that some of the models used by economists may be expressed in mathematical terms. This will be explored in Chapter 8.

The coordination problem

Thinking about the complexities of the world, you might wonder how it is possible to coordinate all the myriad decisions being taken by the multitude of economic agents in a society. This has been one of the challenges that economic analysis has had to face. For example, how are the decisions taken by consumers about what to buy reconciled with the decisions of firms on how much output to produce, and of which goods and services?

In this example, one possible answer is that economic agents respond to signals that they receive. One of the ways in which consumers perceive scarcity is through the fact that they need to pay for goods and services with limited funds available, and that the various goods and services available carry a price. We can view the prices that consumers must pay as being a signal from firms about what they are prepared to provide to the market. At the same time, by observing how much of a good a firm is able to sell at a given price, the firm receives a signal about how much consumers are prepared to pay. If consumers and firms respond to price as a signal, then perhaps some common ground can be found.

From a different perspective, governments may intervene to influence the sorts of goods and services that can be consumed. This may be through regulation, where governments may prohibit the consumption of some goods, such as hard drugs. It may come through discouragement of the consumption of some goods, such as tobacco. It may also be that the government decides to encourage the consumption of some goods, such as museums and art galleries. In extreme cases, governments may force decisions on society by instructing firms what to produce, as may happen where there is central state planning.

Efficiency and equity

Given that resources are scarce, it is important to ensure that they are allocated in the best possible way for society, rather than being wasted. Because of this, a concern of economic analysis is to explore efficiency – in other words, whether resources are being used appropriately.

What do we mean by 'resources' in this context? One way of approaching this is to think about the resources used by a firm as part of its production process. Firms use raw materials, but also need to employ **labour** (workers), **capital** (machines, transport equipment, buildings, etc.) and land. Firms also require management and enterprise (although we could think of these as being particular forms of labour), plus energy. These various inputs into the production process are known as the **factors of production**.

There are two key aspects of efficiency that are important in economics. First, there is the question of whether firms are being efficient in their use of the factors of production. This is the notion of **productive efficiency**, and whether firms are producing at minimum cost. This is related to **productivity**, which is a way of measuring the efficiency of use of the factors of production: for instance, labour productivity measures the quantity of output produced per unit of labour input.

A second important aspect of efficiency is whether firms are producing the appropriate mix of products, in terms of what consumers wish to consume. It would be considered inefficient if firms were to be producing lots of products that consumers did not want to consume. Whether the firms in an economy are producing the best combination of goods and services is known as **allocative efficiency**.

An associated issue is that of equity between individuals and groups within society. In other words, economics is not only about whether the economy produces the appropriate mix of products for society, but is also concerned with the way in which the resources are allocated amongst the people that make up the society. If some members of society are for some reason vulnerable or excluded from society, then some redistribution of resources may be necessary, and economic analysis can help us to understand why this might occur, and what can be done about it.

Where does policy fit in?

So far, the discussion has focused on the subject matter of economics, and an approach to economic analysis based on rational choice, but little has been said about economic policy. If we can understand how the economy works, the question naturally arises as to whether we (via government) can intervene to make it work better.

The role of the economist in policy formulation can be contentious. Economic analysis may enable us to identify the likely effect of a particular policy given assumptions about how economic agents will react to altered signals. This represents a **positive** set of statements, noting that a policy will have a certain set of outcomes. This contrasts with a more **normative** approach, whereby a politician might assert that a certain set of actions *ought* to be taken in order to improve the well-being of society. In other words, the normative approach involves making value judgements about a course of action, whereas as a scientist, the economist may analyse the potential impact of a policy regardless of whether he or she agrees that it should be done.

A way of thinking

Many economics textbooks (and many economists) argue that what sets economics apart from other disciplines is that it provides a particular way of thinking about the world. This chapter has introduced some of the key concepts that underpin that way of thinking. If you choose to pursue a degree programme in economics, you will doubtless meet these concepts and come to appreciate what is meant by this 'way of thinking'. This book will expand upon these key concepts, and show you something of the economist's way of thinking. However, the book will also introduce you to alternative viewpoints and highlight some of the debates and controversies that characterise the way in which non-economists perceive the discipline.

In Chapter 2, we will look more carefully at how these questions have been viewed by economic thinkers as the subject has evolved through time – and at some of the debates that have ensued. In Chapter 7, we will look at alternative forms of economic systems, with governments taking on differing degrees of intervention in the running of the economy.

References

Chang, H-J. (2014) *Economics: The User's Guide*. London: Bloomsbury Press.

Robbins, L. (1932) *An Essay on the Nature and Significance of Economic Science*. London: Macmillan. Available at https://books.google.co.uk/books?id=nySoIkOgWQ4C&printsec=find&pg=PR10&redir_esc=y#v=onepage&q&f=false

Samuelson, P. (1948) *Economics*. New York, NY: McGraw-Hill.

Quality Assurance Agency (QAA) (2015) *Subject Benchmark Statement: Economics*. Part of the UK Quality Code for Higher Education. Available at http://www.qaa.ac.uk/en/Publications/Documents/SBS-Economics-15.pdf

2

The origins and evolution of economic thinking

This chapter will:

- examine the early development of economic ideas and issues
- highlight the key ideas of classical economists
- discuss the emergence of economics as a subject for study, in particular the birth of neoclassical economic thinking
- show how the Great Depression of the 1930s led to the Keynesian revolution
- comment on the importance of data in economics
- note the beginning of a debate on the role of government in society

Economics as a discipline for study is relatively young, unlike philosophy, mathematics or history, which have been developing over the centuries. Nonetheless, thinkers and scholars have always been aware of economic issues and their importance for how society works, even if their writing was not so formally organised into a recognised subject.

This book is not the place to present a detailed analysis of the history of economic thought or to try to provide an in-depth appraisal of the works of the early economists. There will be time and opportunities for you to study this area of economics if you decide to embark on a degree programme in economics. However, what this chapter attempts to do is to outline how economic thinking evolved as a subject for study as societies became more developed and more aware of the importance of economic issues and their impact on people's well-being. Please be aware that this will be a highly selective account, with no attempt to mention everyone who deserves it.

The beginnings

Chapter 1 argued that the need to make choices in the face of scarcity under-pins much of economic analysis, together with Samuelson's three questions. This applies to any social grouping, and as humans began to communicate and cooperate with each other, some of the economic issues that later were to become the subject of study by economists must have emerged.

Imagine a tribe developing as a primitive form of society. Given the inevitable differences between individuals, there would be some who were seen to be relatively good at hunting, whereas other members of the tribe might be better at gathering, cooking or making clothing. Tribal leaders would emerge who would gain status and privilege. To put this in more modern terms, there would be specialisation of tasks, and questions emerging about the distribution of income and wealth.

As groups began to interact with each other, specialisation is likely to have led to the growth of trade and exchange. Being able to trade meat for fish, or cloth for tools would be potentially beneficial for neighbouring groups. Initially, trade would have been carried out through a **barter** system, directly swapping one type of good for another. Barter as the basis for trade is highly inefficient. You need to find someone willing to exchange goods that you want to obtain for goods that you have available to provide – a notion that later came to be called economists by a *double coincidence of wants*.

Glyn Davies (2002) relates an example of how barter could go horribly wrong, which had been set out by Jevons (1875):

> Mlle Zélie, a French opera singer, in the course of a world tour gave a concert in the Society Islands and for her fee received one-third of the proceeds. Her share consisted of three pigs, twenty-three turkeys, forty-five chickens, five thousand coconuts and considerable numbers of bananas, lemons and oranges . . .

In many primitive societies, ownership of cattle became a sign of wealth and prestige, and cattle effectively became a form of currency. Other valued objects, such as cowrie shells or salt, came to be used in trade – effectively a form of money. Indeed, there is evidence that trade was facilitated by the use of some form of money for several thousands of years BCE. Gold bars and rings were used in Egypt and Mesopotamia 3,000 years BCE, and coins were first recorded being used in Turkey and (independently) in China in the seventh to third century BCE (Davies, 2002).

The significance of money for the economy was to become a contentious topic for debate amongst economists in later years. Once money became established as part of how society operates, questions about the role of prices began to emerge – not to mention the issue of **inflation** and its effects on the economy (Box 2.1).

Box 2.1 Inflation and deflation

It is useful at this point to digress to comment on what is meant by inflation, and why it is important.

Inflation is defined as the rate of change of the overall price level in the economy, and from the mid-1970s it became the main target of economic policy at the economy-wide level. As part of your study of economics, you will discover how this came about, and why a high rate of inflation can be damaging for the economy. Even without studying this in detail, imagine how life would be if prices were increasing by several thousand per cent each year. Firms and consumers would not be able to take good decisions because of uncertainty about future prices. There have been episodes in countries in different parts of the world where inflation has got out of control (Germany before the Second World War, Hungary, Latin America in the 1980s or Zimbabwe in more recent years are all examples). Hence the preoccupation with inflation since the 1970s. The opposite situation (**deflation**, when prices fall over time) also creates problems.

Economic history suggests that inflation had not been a major concern of the early economists, if only because it rarely happened, at least on the scale that affected economies in the twentieth century. Inflation (and deflation) had occasionally been discussed (for example, in the time of Henry VIII), but it became a hot topic mainly in the twentieth century.

With the use of money for trade and exchange came the possibility of saving – using money as a store of value. This also raises the possibility of lending and borrowing, with the associated question of whether it was moral to impose a charge for borrowing money in the form of interest. Historically, many of the world's major religions have prohibited the charging of interest, this having been seen as *usury* (the practice of making unethical or immoral monetary loans that provide unfair gains for the lender). For example, charging interest was prohibited in Christianity in the Middle Ages, and is prohibited under Islamic law today.

Another development worthy of note came with the emergence of the nation-state and the monarchy. This required the imposition of taxation to provide funding for the monarch and for the defence of the realm.

These issues all became part of the subject matter of economics once it began to develop as a discipline for study.

Taxation and economic measurement

The question of how to raise finance for wars or other purposes was one of the first economic issues to receive the attention of scholars. One of the earliest writers was the Hampshire-born economist William Petty, writing in the seventeenth century. He had a remarkable life, including being cabin boy, personal secretary to Thomas Hobbes, teaching anatomy at Oxford, travelling with Oliver Cromwell's army in Ireland as physician-general, becoming an MP, being knighted by Charles II and developing an interest in naval architecture.

His economic writings were wide-ranging and influential, although his name is less well known than the economists who were to follow. In particular, he recognised the importance of economic measurement, writing about the need for political arithmetic and providing early estimates of the value of national income and wealth. He has been described as one of England's first statisticians. He also analysed the relative merits of alternative forms of taxation. Many of his ideas appeared in a more systematic form in the later writings of the classical writers such as Adam Smith, David Ricardo and others.

Specialisation and the division of labour

A key figure in the development of economics as a discipline was Adam Smith, whose book *An Inquiry into the Nature and Causes of the Wealth of Nations* (Smith, 1776) was arguably the first major work on economics (or 'political economy' as it would have been known then). This was perhaps the first attempt to draw together economic ideas in a systematic manner, and the book covers a wide range of issues, including ideas about value and prices, and how the self-interest of economic agents could drive the allocation of resources. We will come back to this.

One of the most famous ideas set out in the book was the notion of the **division of labour**. This was seen to operate at two levels.

First, Smith noted that there would be gains for a society when individuals specialise in performing certain functions. For example, it would not make sense for a farmer to perform all the work needed to grow food, and then also to make his own clothes, pots and pans and so on. If people were able to specialise in performing different functions and then engage in a process of exchange this would be much better.

Further, Smith argued that specialisation would also be beneficial within a particular trade or occupation. By separating the production process into stages, and by dividing the labour force between the stages (thus allowing them to specialise), total production could be increased substantially. The extent to which it was possible to benefit from this would be governed by the extent of the market. In other words, it would not pay to use division of labour where the opportunities for trade were limited.

Comparative advantage and trade

David Ricardo also considered questions of specialisation and trade. In *On the Principles of Political Economy and Taxation* (1817) he developed the notion of

comparative advantage, arguing that a country should specialise in the production of goods in which it faced relatively lower production costs, and then engage in trade that would be mutually beneficial to both trading partners. In this, he supported Adam Smith in his arguments against protectionism.

Ricardo used a now-famous numerical example, in which England and Portugal were each capable of producing cloth and wine. Portugal could produce both goods using less labour than England, but was relatively better at producing wine. In economist-speak, Portugal had an **absolute advantage** in the production of both goods, but a comparative advantage in producing wine. If each country were to specialise in the good in which they had a comparative advantage (Portugal in wine and England in cloth) then trade could leave both countries better off. (This example was later to be disputed by Joan Robinson (1933).)

Diminishing returns and the distribution of income

Ricardo believed that the agricultural sector faced diminishing returns. In other words, as the sector expanded, more intensive use would need to be made of already-cultivated land, and less productive land would be drawn into production. Thus the additional produce that could be gained by expanding would diminish. This in turn would affect the rent on land and the way in which income was distributed between labourers, capitalists (the owners of capital) and landlords. In particular, higher rents would redistribute income in favour of the landlords, and away from the capitalists, thus stifling investment and innovation, as the landlords would squander their income on luxury goods (Box 2.2).

Box 2.2 The law of diminishing marginal returns

There are very few 'laws' in economics, unlike in subjects such as physics. An important law is the **law of diminishing marginal returns**.

Suppose that a firm employs more labour without also expanding the input of other factors of production. The law states that the extra output produced by the additional labour will fall. This makes sense intuitively: if the extra workers have to share the same capital equipment, or if additional agricultural labourers work the same amount of land, their productivity is likely to fall, as they will be competing to use the same machinery or will get in each other's way.

A subsistence wage?

At this time, it was widely believed that the value of goods reflected the labour used in producing them. Adam Smith had argued this in the *Wealth of Nations*, and this was reinforced by other writers, including Ricardo, who termed this the labour theory of value.

Thomas Malthus (1798) had put forward the idea that although population grew exponentially, food production could only grow arithmetically. Population growth would put increasing pressure on food production. Combined with diminishing returns, there would be famines, disease and wars, so that wages would always return to some subsistence level. Ideas that run along these lines are still current today.

These so-called 'Classical' writers were thus basically pessimistic about the prospects for **economic growth**, as diminishing returns would always force the economy back to a subsistence level wage (Box 2.3).

Box 2.3 Economic growth

Economic growth here refers to the expansion in total output in an economy from one period to the next. This will be explored more fully later in the book.

Karl Marx (1867) interpreted Ricardo's labour theory of value in a new way, arguing that capitalists would alienate labour by usurping part of the value of the goods that they produced. Capitalists would squeeze the labour share, and production would come to be concentrated in large firms, which would utilise more capital to avoid pressure from labour. Profits would fall, because although labour produces surplus value, capital does not (in Marx's view). Capitalism would thus move from crisis to crisis until revolution would herald a new era. Thus Marx believed that capitalism would eventually be destroyed, to be replaced by socialism, which would eventually give way to communism.

The coordination problem revisited

No account of the early writings of the Classical economists would be complete without some comment about issues of resource allocation. How would an economic system work towards allocating resources in response to competing demands? Adam Smith's answer was that the self-interest of individuals and firms would bring about an allocation of resources that was good for society, even if this was not intended. He referred to this as the operation of an **'invisible hand'**:

As every individual, therefore, endeavours as much as he can both to employ his capital in the support of domestic industry, and so to direct that industry that its produce may be of the greatest value; every individual necessarily labours to render the annual revenue of the society as great as he can. He generally, indeed, neither intends to promote the public interest, nor knows how much he is promoting it . . . by directing that industry in such a manner as its produce may be of the greatest value, he intends only his own gain, and he is in this, as in many other cases, led by an invisible hand to promote an end which was no part of his intention . . . By pursuing his own interest he frequently promotes that of the society more effectually than when he really intends to promote it.

Smith (1776, IV.2.9)

Smith was aware that there could be situations in which individuals or firms might collude together to distort the way in which resources are distributed, but the overall message that comes through is that the invisible hand will guide the overall allocation of resources.

The birth of neoclassical economics

Towards the end of the nineteenth century economic thinking moved in a new direction, as scholars began to apply mathematical techniques to study economic issues. Prominent here were writers such as Léon Walras (a French economist based in Switzerland) and Vilfredo Pareto, an Italian who succeeded to Walras's chair at the University of Lausanne. Pareto was trained as an engineer, but then applied his training to the study of economics. In economics, Pareto is best known for the concept of **Pareto optimality** (or **Pareto efficiency**). This was the idea that the best allocation of resources for a society would occur if no reallocation could make someone better off without making somebody else worse off.

A significant milestone in the development of economics as a subject was the publication of Alfred Marshall's *Principles of Economics* in 1890, which was to have a major influence on the profession. Indeed, the book marked the period in which the word 'economics' replaced 'political economy' as the name of the subject.

Marshall read mathematics at Cambridge, and when he came to write about economics he wanted to use the language to which he was accustomed – mathematical equations and diagrams. This became the accepted approach for economic analysis, both for teaching and research.

In the *Principles*, Marshall introduced some of the diagrams that still feature in textbooks today, such as the demand and supply diagram (which we will meet in the next chapter), together with many other tools that have now become a standard part of the economist's armoury.

Marshall did not simply translate existing economic ideas into mathematical or diagrammatic form. Together with other economists, such as Jevons, he moved away from the pessimism of the Classical writers, heralding what is now known as **neoclassical economics**. This approach embodied a more smooth and harmonious process that could result in expansion of production over time. The neoclassical view recognised the possibility of technological progress, which could help to overcome the problem of diminishing returns. Capital played a more active role, with the possibility of substituting for labour, not forcing labour into unemployment or reduced to the subsistence wage, but releasing labour for more productive uses, complementing the expansion of capital. In addition, the notion that prices could guide resource allocation came to the fore, giving substance to the working of Smith's invisible hand.

Marshall championed the idea that economic agents would seek to act rationally, having a clear objective and seeking to maximise it. In particular, it was argued that individuals would set out to maximise utility (as mentioned in Chapter 1). This notion of rational economic agents was to dominate much economic thinking during the early part of the twentieth century and beyond.

The use of scientific tools such as mathematics and diagrams created the sense that economics could be viewed as a 'science' that could provide a definitive explanation of the decisions of economic agents and the operation of markets. Whether economics should be regarded as a science will be explored in Chapter 6.

The idea that prices would adjust to bring about a balance in a market between what people wanted to buy and what firms wanted to sell suggested that the government could take a relatively passive role and allow market forces to allocate resources effectively. To put this another way, if all markets were to work perfectly, society would find that resources were allocated in such a way as to achieve Pareto optimality. Government should adopt a *laissez-faire* (hands-off) approach to the economy – a phrase coined much earlier in favour of minimalist government intervention.

Imperfect competition

Would markets work perfectly?

Many writers had recognised early that markets might not always work in the perfect way that the neoclassical economists discussed. The notion that firms might collude had been set out in Adam Smith's *Wealth of Nations*, as noted in Chapter 1. In the nineteenth century, Antoine Augustin Cournot in 1838 had discussed a model in which a market was supplied by two firms (a **duopoly**), discussing how each firm would react to the output decisions taken by the other firm. In 1883, Jean Bertrand proposed an alternative model in which firms reacted to the price set by other firms. These models can be seen as the precursors of **game theory**, in which the way in which a market operates is examined by considering alternative strategies that firms could adopt.

In the period between the two World Wars, the question of whether markets would work perfectly aroused much debate. Writers like Joan Robinson (1933) in England and Edward Chamberlin (1933) in the USA argued that there was a variety of ways in which a market could be structured other than being either a **monopoly** (a market in which there is only one seller) or the perfect competition envisaged by Pareto and Marshall.

The Great Depression

The *laissez-faire* approach to governing the economy was dramatically thrown into question by the events of the 1920s and 1930s, as illustrated in Figure 2.1, which shows the **unemployment rate** in the UK since 1920 (Box 2.4).

Box 2.4 Unemployment rate

For an economy, the unemployment rate is defined as the percentage of those available for work and wanting to work who are unemployed – that is, people who are neither employed nor self-employed but would like to be.

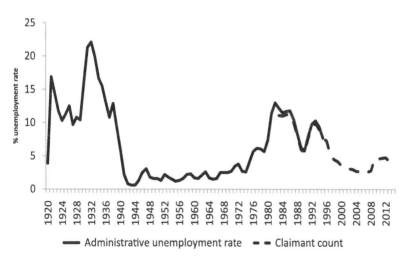

Figure 2.1 The unemployment rate in the UK since 1920 (*Sources:* Adapted from data from the Office for National Statistics licensed under the Open Government Licence v.3.0. Administrative unemployment rate from Labour Market Trends January 1996. Claimant count from ONS Labour Market Statistics).

You can see from the figure that unemployment had been high in the after-math of the First World War, reaching 17% in 1921. Although the rate then fell as the economy recovered, the Great Crash of 1929 saw unemployment rise to more than 20% in 1931 and 1932, with only a gradual recovery.

Belief in the neoclassical view that markets would adjust discouraged the government from intervening, except by trying to reduce wages in the hope that this would encourage firms to employ more labour. In fact, it was only with the outset of the Second World War that unemployment fell significantly, as the unemployed were taken into military service.

The Keynesian Revolution

The most influential economist of the twentieth century was John Maynard Keynes. His book *The General Theory of Employment, Interest and Money*, published in 1936, launched what is now known as 'macroeconomics'. The main focus of economics until that time had been the economic decision-making of individual economic agents – households and firms. Keynes explored the relationships between economic variables at the *aggregate* level – in other words, at the level of the economy as a whole. This was partly in response to the high levels of unemployment in the 1930s, which had not only affected the UK, but were also evident across the developed world (Box 2.5).

Box 2.5 Economic variables

When we are talking about the economy as a whole, there are some key things such as inflation, unemployment or economic growth that vary through time. Economists refer to these as *variables*.

Keynes argued that the unemployment had resulted from low levels of overall effective demand ('aggregate demand') in the economy, and that the government could have been more active in stimulating demand, allowing the economy to recover more quickly.

Keynes's ideas provoked much debate amongst economists, and opened up a new way of thinking about economics. This also led to a fundamental change in the approach to the design of economic policy. No longer would the economy be left to find its own way, but governments were now seen to be in a position to influence the course of the economy through time.

Keynes was active politically, and played a key role in the conference held at Bretton Woods in 1944, which set out to design a system that would establish a new international framework for the monetary and financial order. One aspect of this was to establish an exchange rate regime in which most economies tied their exchange rate to the US dollar, the so-called **dollar standard**. In addition, three important multilateral organisations were established that would shape the post-war global economy. The **International Monetary Fund (IMF)** would take responsibility for stability of exchange rates, being ready to make loans to countries that were facing difficulties in maintaining the value of their currency. The **World Bank** would be responsible for providing loans for long-term development programmes. The **General Agreement on Tariffs and Trade (GATT)** took responsibility for regulating international trade, with a specific brief to oversee a programme of tariff reductions. This responsibility has now been given to the **World Trade Organisation (WTO)**.

Economics and data

The focus on the aggregate economy brought with it the need to monitor the performance of the economy, which required improved measurement of economic aggregates. William Petty had tried to estimate national income in the seventeenth century, but Keynes had now provided a structure for thinking about the concept more systematically. In the aftermath of the Second World War, it was now possible to measure key economic variables more reliably and systematically.

Statistical methods had also developed significantly since Petty's early attempts, and a new branch of economic analysis came into being – **econometrics**. This was the application of mathematics and statistics to explore economic phenomena – and to test whether economic theories were consistent with what was happening in the real world. If you choose to study an undergraduate degree programme in economics, you are likely to be introduced to techniques of econometrics.

The role of government

Since the end of the Second World War, there has been much debate about the role of government in seeking to influence the path of the economy. This partly reflected the influence of Keynes, with his argument that a government could influence the level of aggregate demand, and thus stabilise the economy. It was also stimulated by the Cold War, and the contrast that could be seen between the state planning of countries in the Communist world, and the approach taken in the West, where governments were active in the economy, but were intervening in the context of a market-driven economy.

In the developed economies of the West, cracks began to appear as time went by, with inflation accelerating in the late 1960s, resulting in the abandonment of the dollar standard in the early 1970s. At this point in time, some neoclassical ideas began to reappear.

In addition, it was rapidly becoming apparent that there were many countries, especially in sub-Saharan Africa but also in parts of Asia and Latin America, that were being left behind in terms of economic growth, with an enormous gap in living standards opening up. Concerns were also growing about the need to safeguard the environment, with reserves of key commodities threatening to be exhausted. Technology was changing at an unprecedented rate, raising new questions about economic processes. Financial systems were also changing rapidly.

With all these things coming together, the relationship between government and economy was also changing. Economic thinking evolved further, interacting with policy design. New theories led to new policy proposals, and new problems brought developments in economic theory. Chapter 5 will return to these developments, after some key ideas have been introduced.

References

Chamberlin, E. (1933) *The Theory of Monopolistic Competition*. Cambridge, MA: Harvard University Press.

Davies, G. (2002) *A History of Money: from Ancient Times to the Present Day*. Cardiff: University of Wales Press.

Jevons, W.S. (1875) *Money and the Mechanism of Exchange*. London: C. Kegan Paul. Available at http://www.econlib.org/library/YPDBooks/Jevons/jvnMME1.html#firstpage-bar

Malthus, T.R. (1798) *An Essay on the Principle of Population*. London: J. Johnson.

Marx, K. (1867) *Das Kapital*, Volume 1. Available at https://www.marxists.org/archive/marx/works/1867-c1/

Ricardo, D. (1817) *On the Principles of Political Economy and Taxation*. London: John Murray.

Robinson, J. (1933) *The Economics of Imperfect Competition*. London: Macmillan.

Smith, A. (1776) *An Inquiry into the Nature and Causes of the Wealth of Nations*. London: Methuen & Co. Available at http://www.econlib.org/library/Smith/smWN.html

PART II

The scope of economics

Micro and macro perspectives

This chapter will:

- highlight the distinction between microeconomics and macroeconomics
- introduce the demand and supply model and the key notion of equilibrium
- explain how the model enables analysis of how markets adjust to changes in market conditions
- discuss how markets may fail to produce a good outcome for society
- note that there may be situations in which economic agents may not act rationally
- introduce key aspects of macroeconomic thinking
- identify macroeconomic policy objectives and instruments

Chapter 2 discussed how economics developed as a subject, initially mainly focusing on decisions made by individual economic agents until Keynes drew attention to the need to consider how the economy as a whole operates.

This highlights a distinction between **macroeconomics** (the study of interactions between economic variables at the aggregate level) and **microeconomics** (the study of the economic behaviour of individual economic agents). This distinction remains in many (if not most) university degree programmes, although it is recognised that there are common approaches and ways of thinking used in both, and that much macroeconomic analysis builds upon microeconomic principles.

Although this book is not intended to be a textbook, this chapter introduces some of the key terms and concepts used in both microeconomics and macroeconomics, and how these are analysed by economists. This should give you a flavour of what to expect on your degree programme. We begin with microeconomics.

Microeconomics

The focus of microeconomics is on studying the economic behaviour of individual economic agents, and how this shapes decision-making. Initially, we will consider decisions taken by consumers (who buy goods and services) and firms (which supply goods and services). This takes us to what is probably the most famous of all models in economics – the demand and supply model. This will be used to introduce the way in which economists work.

Demand

Most microeconomics textbooks begin by analysing demand and supply, albeit in varying levels of detail. Here, we will just try to capture the essence of the approach, and explain what it reveals about how markets work.

As an example, think about the demand for and the supply of ice cream. Consumers of ice cream and the firms that supply it interact in the context of a **market**. When economists talk about a market, they mean any set of arrangements that enables transactions to take place. This need not (but could be) a physical location, such as the local farmers' market or the stock exchange. However, it could also encompass online arrangements for buying and selling.

The 'demand' side of the demand and supply model captures the fact that there are consumers who wish to buy a good or service being traded in a market. The key question is what are the factors that influence consumers in their decision on whether to buy a particular good, and in what quantity?

Returning to the example of ice cream, think for a moment about what factors affect *your* demand for ice cream. There are likely to be a number of influences. Perhaps you will consider the price of ice cream, and the money you have in your pocket that you could spend. You might also think about alternative products that might tempt you. Perhaps you quite fancy a latté or an espresso, but do not have enough cash for both coffee and an ice cream? It may be a hot day that adds to the temptation of buying an ice cream? Maybe you don't like ice cream anyway?

To make sense of all these elements, some structure needs to be imposed on things. In order to organise the influences, economists tend to categorise the factors into four key influences:

- the price of ice cream
- consumer income/budget
- the price of other goods
- consumer preferences.

The next step is to introduce an assumption. It turns out that in order for the demand and supply model to be helpful, it is useful to focus on the relationship between the demand for a good and its price, *assuming* that all the other factors are fixed.

Again if you think about this, you will almost certainly be more likely to buy an ice cream when the price is relatively low than when it is relatively expensive. Furthermore, if you have already just had an ice cream, even a low price may not induce you to have another one. This suggests that there is a negative relationship between your demand for ice cream and the price at which it is selling – remembering that other influences on the decision are being assumed constant.

In the market as a whole, most consumers are likely to think in the same way, although some may place different valuations on the consumption of ice cream. This suggests that for the market as a whole, a higher quantity will be demanded when the price is relatively low than when the price is high. This can be represented in a diagram, as shown in Figure 3.1.

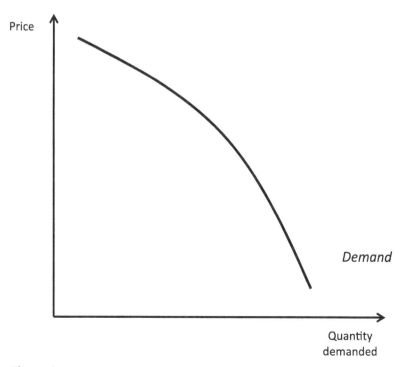

Figure 3.1 **A demand curve.**

You will find that economists use diagrams frequently, as they can be useful in analysis. In this case, the price of a good is measured (or portrayed) on the vertical axis, and the quantity demanded is on the horizontal axis. (This is the way that Alfred Marshall drew the demand curve in his *Principles*, and has been the pattern ever since.) Reading the diagram is a key skill for economic analysis. The fact that the **demand curve** is drawn to be downward sloping confirms that there is a negative relationship between the price of the good and the quantity demanded. At a relatively high price, the quantity demanded is relatively low, but as the price falls, so more is demanded.

Supply

The power of the demand and supply model comes into play when we add to this some similar reasoning about how firms take decisions about how much to supply. There are a number of factors that will influence the quantity of a good (or service) that firms will be prepared to supply to the market. For a start, they will take into account the price that they can receive for selling the good. They will also consider the cost of producing the good, and the potential profits that could be made from producing something else instead, and so on.

As with the analysis of demand, the next step is to focus on the relationship between the quantity that firms will wish to supply and the price that they can obtain for the good. This time, it would be expected that (other things being equal), firms would be prepared to supply a higher quantity when the price is relatively high. In other words, there is likely to be a *positive* relationship between the price of a good and the quantity that firms are prepared to supply. Such a **supply curve** is added to the demand curve in Figure 3.2.

Equilibrium

This may not seem to have taken us very far, but we now have a framework that will allow us to analyse this market and make some useful statements about how the market will work in practice. This relies on thinking about different locations in the diagram. Figure 3.3 identifies some alternative scenarios.

Think about what would happen if the price were to be at a relatively high level such as P_1. Consumers would be prepared to demand the quantity Q_x, but firms would be prepared to supply Q_y. What would then happen is that firms would find that they could not sell as much as they would like to, and they would be left with unsold goods. In response, they would be likely to reduce the quantity supplied and reduce the price. As the price fell, consumers would demand more, moving down along the demand curve.

On the other hand, if the price were to be set as low as P_2, the opposite situation would occur: consumers would not be able to obtain as much of the good

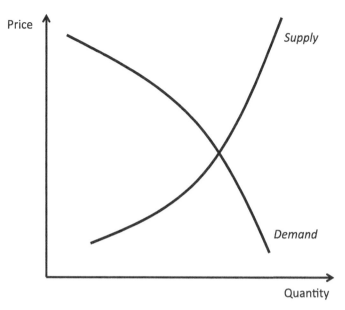

Figure 3.2 Demand and supply.

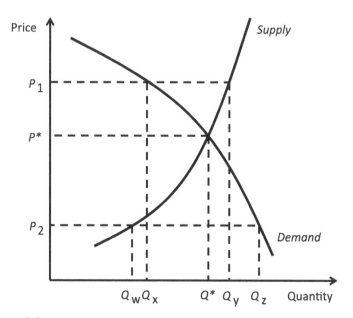

Figure 3.3 Demand and supply equilibrium.

as they would like to demand at that price, so would begin to bid up the price, inducing firms to supply more, moving along their supply curve.

The point at which things would settle down would be when the price reached P^*, at which consumers demand Q^* and firms supply Q^*. This is an **equilibrium** point, where there is a balance between demand and supply.

This is what is meant when people say that the price of a good is determined by demand and supply – it is the price that brings consistency between what consumers wish to buy and firms wish to sell.

Changes in the equilibrium position

You might interrupt here, and point out that this all depends upon the assumption that was made that the other factors that influence both demand and supply had been assumed to be unchanged. And you would be quite correct. However, that is where the usefulness of the model comes into play, because we can now see how the market reacts if any of those things change.

For example, suppose that the government suddenly decides that eating ice cream is bad for you, and mounts a campaign that highlights the dangers of eating too much ice cream. This may deter some people from eating ice cream. In other words, for any given price, there will be lower demand for ice cream. In terms of the diagram, this means that the demand curve will shift to the left, as in Figure 3.4, where demand shifts from D_0 to D_1.

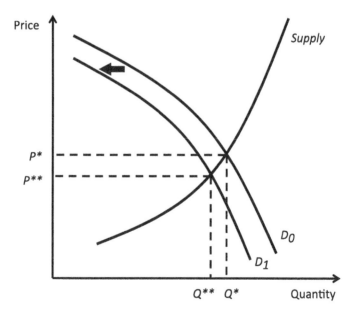

Figure 3.4 **A change in demand.**

You can see that there would be a change in the equilibrium position, with price falling to P^{**} and quantity traded increasing to Q^{**}.

Similarly, if one of the factors that influences supply changes – for example, if there is an increase in firms' costs – then the supply curve would shift, and the market would move to a new equilibrium.

Another important observation here is that the extent to which price and quantity change in response to a shift in one of the curves depends upon the relative shapes of the curves. For example, the degree to which demand is sensitive to price reflects the shape and slope of the demand curve, and on the initial price. The degree of sensitivity is measured by the **price elasticity of demand**, which you will no doubt meet early on in your study of economics.

When the percentage change in quantity demanded is greater than the percentage change in price that brought it about, we refer to demand as being *elastic*. If a firm increases its price when demand is elastic, the resulting fall in sales will more than offset the price increase, so the firm's revenue from sales will fall. Knowing that demand is elastic may therefore deter a firm from raising price. The intuition here is that firms may not be able to raise price when their customers are sensitive to the price. If the reverse is the case, demand is said to be inelastic, and an increase in price will lead to a relatively small decrease in demand.

Notice that the model is also based on the assumption that consumers and firms are behaving in such a way as to maximise their objectives. Consumers act to maximise their utility (as explained in Chapter 1), and firms act to maximise their profits. If firms find that they could make more profit in a different market, they may choose to move out of this current business. If this happened, then the market supply curve would shift to the left, and the equilibrium price would increase. Similarly if firms not in the market see that this is potentially more profitable, then they will enter, shifting the supply curve to the right, resulting in a lower equilibrium price. In this way, prices act as signals to producers that guide them into the most profitable markets. It is in this sense that prices guide the allocation of resources between alternative products.

This illustrates how economists can use a simple model to analyse how the market for a good (or service) will operate, reaching an equilibrium position in a variety of circumstances, and influencing the overall allocation of resources.

Do markets always work like this?

The demand and supply model described above is a simplified version of a competitive market as set out by Marshall, which Pareto argued would lead to an allocation of resources which was beneficial to society. But will markets always operate in this convenient way? If only life was so simple. In practice, there may be many reasons why markets may not be so perfect.

One way in which markets may not be perfect is where firms are able to exert some market power. If there is a monopoly, or if there are just a few firms (an **oligopoly**) that are able to collude together to influence the market, then they may be able to tilt the scales in their favour and increase their profits at the expense of consumers. In the UK, the **Competition and Markets Authority (CMA)** has been set up to monitor markets to see that consumers are protected from anti-competitive action taken by firms.

When there are just a few firms operating in a market, it is much more difficult to analyse how the market will develop. Game theory is widely used in analysing the strategies that firms may adopt when trying to influence the behaviour of their rivals, or how they will react to actions taken by other firms.

If you choose to study economics, you will meet a number of other circumstances in which markets will fail to produce this ideal outcome for society. One such situation is where firms in a market impose costs such as pollution on society without having to meet the costs of doing so. Economists refer to this as an **externality**, where firms impose costs on other economic agents, and thus produce more output than is good for society. This explains why governments introduce taxes or regulations in order to control the emission of pollutants. Notice that where the effects of pollution cross international borders, it may be difficult to regulate. When airports in Singapore and Malaysia are forced to close because of haze resulting from forest fires in neighbouring Indonesia, this can cause international political debate.

Markets may also fail because of the characteristics of some goods. For example, who should pay for street lighting or national defence? Private firms are unlikely to provide these goods, because what member of the public would be willing to pay for them? After all, as soon as one person has paid for the good, everyone else could benefit without paying – so why should anyone be the first to pay! This is known as the **free-rider problem**.

There are also markets where problems can arise from a lack of information, or where some partners to a transaction have better information than others. If some economic agents have better information than others, they may be able to exploit this to their own advantage. In some cases this may destroy a market altogether. Suppose an individual goes to the bank to ask for a loan for a project. The bank may not be able to come to a clear view of the riskiness of the project – and the borrower will know more. The bank may thus demand a higher rate of interest on the loan. Borrowers with a low-risk project will not perceive this as fair, so only high-risk borrowers may agree to the bank's terms, and the bank is left with loans with a high risk of failure. This has been an important problem in some less-developed countries, where potential borrowers (especially in rural areas) have been unable to obtain credit from the formal financial sector, and have been forced to borrow from local moneylenders who are able to charge punitive rates of interest.

These are among the many issues that you will learn about if you choose to pursue study in economics.

Do economic agents always act rationally?

Do firms always set out to maximise profits? And do consumers always set out to maximise their utility?

The behaviour of firms and consumers does not suggest that they always pursue a maximisation objective. Firms may be more concerned about market share or growth. This may be especially so when a firm becomes large, so that the ownership of the firm is separated from the managers who take the day-to-day decisions. Consumers may buy goods that are on 'special offer' or carefully displayed near the supermarket exit, rather than by thinking rationally about what would bring them most utility, or they may act from humanitarian motives. These are also issues that you are likely to meet on an economics programme.

Macroeconomics

Macroeconomics studies the economy at the aggregate level, looking at the relationships between economic variables. A starting point in exploring this is to consider how it is possible to measure the total resources being produced in an economy. In principle, there are three ways in which this can be done – by calculating the total output being produced, by observing the total spending being undertaken, or by the total incomes being paid to residents of the country. If we were to measure things accurately, the answer should be the same whichever approach is adopted, but in practice there is always a statistical discrepancy.

Gross domestic product

The answer to these calculations is known as **gross domestic product (GDP)**. This represents the total amount of economic activity that takes place in the domestic economy in a period of time. It is useful to begin by considering the expenditure method of measuring GDP, as this tells us how the resources in the economy are being used.

The various expenditures that take place can be categorised into a few key components. Households buy goods and services to consume. This is the largest part of expenditure, and is known as **consumption (C)**. Firms buy machinery, transport equipment and other items of capital goods in order to undertake production. This is known as **investment (I)**, and must not be confused with the activity by which people buy financial assets. This is some-times known as 'investment' from the perspective of the individual, but is not what is meant in this context. Governments also undertake spending on goods and services **(Government expenditure (G))**. International trade also needs to be taken into account. **Exports (X)** represents spending by the rest of the world on domestically produced goods and services. However, some spending by domestic residents is on goods produced elsewhere, so **imports (M)** need to be deducted from the total.

This can be expressed in a simple equation:

$$GDP = C + I + G + (X - M)$$

You may sometimes come across another indicator of total incomes in a country known as **gross national income (GNI)**. Indeed, this is used as a standard measure for comparing average incomes between countries. This is GDP adjusted for net income from abroad. This reflects the way that some people (such as migrant workers) may work in one country but remit part of their income to families abroad. This has been important for some less-developed countries where workers have gone to work abroad and remit some of their income back home to their families.

Aggregate demand

It is also possible to view these components of GDP as being the components of **aggregate demand**, and this in turn can be seen as a starting point for the approach to macroeconomics that was initiated by Keynes. In his *General Theory*, Keynes looked at how the components of aggregate demand were determined, and what this implied for the path followed by the economy.

One of the key notions that Keynes developed was that households would face a choice on how to allocate their income between consumption expenditure and saving. He argued that faced with an increase in income at their disposal, households would devote part to consumption and part to saving. The proportion of additional income that would be devoted to consumption is the **marginal propensity to consume**.

As far as investment is concerned, Keynes argued that a key determinant would be the 'animal spirits' of firms and entrepreneurs. This could deepen periods of recession, as if firms held pessimistic expectations about the future course of the economy, they would not be prepared to undertake investment. On the other hand, if firms are optimistic about the future, they may push the economy into a boom.

The key point of departure for Keynes compared to previous writers was that these elements of aggregate demand would determine the state in which the economy would settle, whereas previously it was assumed that it was

aggregate supply that was important. In other words, macroeconomic equilibrium would be determined by the state of aggregate demand. This reflected the view of the classical economists, who argued that supply would create its own demand (Say's Law).

In the context of the Great Depression, Keynes took the view that the economy could settle in an equilibrium that was below the potential level at which resources in the economy would be fully employed. In other words, macroeconomic equilibrium could be at a level in which there was unemployment.

This then opened the possibility for the government to intervene to make up the deficiency in aggregate demand. Furthermore, Keynes argued that an increase in government expenditure would have a multiplied effect on aggregate demand, thus introducing the notion of the **multiplier**. The idea behind this is that if the government increase expenditure, this requires firms to hire more workers, who then spend their income, requiring firms to hire yet more workers . . . and so on. The size of this multiplier effect would be weakened if households have a low marginal propensity to consume, because in each round there would be leakage from the system in the form of savings.

These ideas held sway in the period following the Second World War, with governments in the UK and elsewhere adopting a Keynesian approach in trying to guide the economy. Chapter 5 will discuss how this began to break down as rising inflation threatened to destabilise the economy, and competing theories emerged.

Macroeconomic policy objectives

Keynes had planted the idea that governments could exert more control of the path of the economy. But what should be the main objectives of policy?

Full employment

In the immediate post-war period, a preoccupation of policy at the macroeconomic level was to avoid the high levels of unemployment that had been prevalent before the war (as was shown in Figure 2.1). **Full employment** was thus a high priority, seen as achieving a level of economic activity in which labour was as fully utilised as possible. This would not mean that unemployment would be zero, as there would always be some workers in the process of moving between jobs.

Stable inflation

The control of inflation became a key objective of macroeconomic policy in the late 1970s. Inflation is defined as the rate of change of the overall price level, measured in the UK by changes in the consumer price index (CPI).

There are several arguments that suggest that a high and volatile rate of inflation may be damaging for the economy, but the main one is that if firms cannot predict the future rate of inflation they will form pessimistic expectations about the course of the economy, which may discourage investment. Figure 3.5 shows the rate of inflation since 1860, showing some interesting patterns.

Notice that for several decades before the First World War inflation had been low, so had not been of major concern to the government. It took off during the war in the face of high military spending, but then became deflation (falling prices) in the 1920s and 1930s during the Great Depression. The Second World War saw another acceleration in inflation, followed by a period of relative stability during the 1950s and 1960s. Inflation then became a serious focus of policy with the acceleration in the 1970s. This triggered a rethinking of macroeconomic theory and policy (see Chapter 5).

The balance of payments

The **balance of payments** is a set of accounts that sets out the transactions that take place between a country and the rest of the world. You may have seen in media discussions that commentators tend to highlight when there is a deficit on the balance of payments. What they really mean by this is that there is a deficit on the **current account of the balance of payments**, which is the section of the accounts that highlights the transactions in goods and services between the country and the rest of the world. When imports exceed exports, this can result in a deficit on the current account, which is sometimes

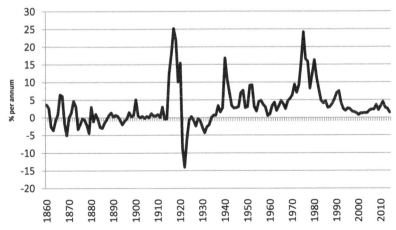

Figure 3.5 Inflation in the UK since 1860 (*Source:* Drawn from data in Hills, S. Thomas, R. and Dimsdale, N. (2015) Three Centuries of Data – Version 2.1, Bank of England).

interpreted as saying that the country is not paying its way, in the sense that it is spending more on importing goods (and services) from abroad than it is receiving from selling its goods (and services). In practice, the current account for the UK has been in deficit in every year since 1984. Whether this matters or not depends partly on how the foreign exchange rate is determined, as you will no doubt discover during your undergraduate studies.

The other accounts that make up the balance of payments are the *financial account*, which brings together transactions in financial assets between the domestic economy and the rest of the world, and the *capital account*, which summarises the transactions in physical capital (mainly the fixed assets of migrants. If there is a deficit on the current account, this must be balanced by a surplus of the financial account, so that the overall balance of payments is zero. In other words, if a country imports more than it exports, it must pay for the difference by selling financial assets.

A current account deficit did matter during the 1950s and 1960s, when the UK was fixing its exchange rate against the US$ as part of the dollar standard. In this period, the economy went through a 'stop–go' cycle. Every time that the economy began to expand, imports rose, pushing the current account of the balance of payments further into deficit, and causing the government to slow the economy down. This was necessary because the deficit had to be covered by using up reserves of foreign exchange.

Economic growth

The most fundamental policy objective for any government is to achieve economic growth – an expansion in the output of the economy through time. Economic growth expands the resources available to citizens of the country, and allows improvements in the standard of living. Policies for creating full employment, low inflation and stability in the balance of payments are all basically aimed at enabling economic growth to take place.

Other objectives

There may be other objectives for policy, such as ensuring an acceptable distribution of income between groups in society. In recent decades, there has also been a concern with protecting the environment, which may sometimes conflict with policies that are aimed at achieving economic growth.

Policy instruments: microeconomic

Policies at the microeconomic level are those that are used to affect individual markets. For example, taxes and subsidies may be used to affect spending on certain products.

In some cases, the government may wish to discourage the consumption of certain products, such as tobacco. Taxes levied on the sale of cigarettes are one way of achieving this. Taxes may also be used in the presence of externalities, for example to discourage firms from emitting pollution. On the other hand, subsidies may be used to encourage consumption of goods that the government perceive to be under-consumed or under-produced.

An alternative is to use direct regulation. An example of this is the banning of smoking in public buildings, or pollution controls that are based on limiting the amount of pollution that is permitted.

The work of the Competition and Markets Authority mentioned earlier is an intervention to protect consumers from exploitation by firms with market power. Governments may also take action to encourage firms to undertake research and development, or to locate in parts of the country where unemployment is persistently high. This is discussed more fully in Chapter 4.

These are all actions that affect the distribution of resources or correct forms of market failure. The extent to which they are effective in achieving these goals is another topic that you are likely to explore as part of your degree programme in economics.

Policy instruments: macroeconomic

Policies that are intended to affect the whole economy rather than particular markets are aimed either at aggregate demand or at aggregate supply.

Fiscal policy

Fiscal policy measures affect aggregate demand through changes in the government's expenditure and taxation. If the authorities wish to stimulate aggregate demand, this can be achieved either by expanding expenditure or by reducing taxation. This could then have Keynesian multiplier effects. However, there are limits to how effective such an approach can be, because of the interaction with the price level. Too much use of fiscal policy to stimulate aggregate demand can lead to upward pressure on prices, thus resulting in inflation. This provoked much debate, as will be seen in Chapter 5.

The fiscal actions of the government can also have an impact on the overall balance of the economy, increasing the public sector at the expense of private sector activity.

Monetary policy is the use of monetary instruments such as the interest rate or the quantity of money in order to influence aggregate demand. During your studies, you will find that the quantity of money in circulation (known as the **money supply**) is one potential instrument of monetary policy. The central bank (the Bank of England in the UK) can influence the money supply, but cannot determine it with precision, because modern financial markets provide many ways in which banks and other financial institutions can create money or credit.

Because of this, the **interest rate** became the favoured instrument of monetary policy in recent decades. When Tony Blair came into power in 1997, one of the first measures that was introduced was to delegate to the Bank of England the responsibility for monetary policy, and this has continued to the present day.

The government sets a target for the inflation rate, and the Bank then sets **bank rate** in order to meet that target. (Bank rate is an interest rate that is set by the Bank of England that influences the rates of interest set by other financial institutions.) If inflation threatens to go above the target, the Bank can raise bank rate, and thus other interest rates, which will discourage firms from spending on investment and households from spending on consumer goods. This reduces the pressure on prices coming from aggregate demand. This approach seemed to be highly successful during the 2000s until the financial crisis that hit towards the end of that decade. The next chapter explores this.

As their name suggests, **supply-side policies** are aimed at affecting aggregate supply. These include measures to improve the efficiency of markets, for example by making labour markets more flexible. There is an overlap here with microeconomic policies, which may also influence aggregate supply – such as measures to encourage firms to undertake research and development.

Alongside these policy instruments, governments may also introduce policies intended to affect the distribution of incomes within society to protect poor and vulnerable members of society. In some of these areas, a careful balance has to be maintained between providing support for the unemployed and providing incentives to work. If social security benefits are too generous, there may be people who will choose not to work.

Designing policy is a major challenge for any government, and at the end of the day it is important to remember that a country like the UK is part of the global economy. It is all too easy to blame a government for poor handling of the economy in the face of changes to the global economic environment that affect many countries simultaneously.

4

Competition and market failure

This chapter will:

- highlight the perceived importance of competition for the economy
- outline the structure–conduct–performance paradigm and the need for the control of market dominance by monopoly firms
- discuss how the internal organisation of firms may affect decisions because of the principal-agent problem
- comment on the strategic interaction between firms
- introduce the notions of nationalisation and privatisation
- identify sources of market failure, including asymmetric information and pollution

Market failure is a key concept in economic analysis. Chapter 3 highlighted the way in which resources could be allocated in an ideal way for society if only there was to be perfect competition in all markets, with prices acting as signals to firms and consumers in order to bring this about. However, this only produces the best results if there are no market imperfections. The implication of this approach is that the role of government is to ensure that markets work as effectively as possible, only intervening where there is some sort of **market failure**.

The pursuit of competition

Patently, the real world is not perfect. For a start, conditions of monopoly and imperfect competition characterise many (if not most) markets. The question that then arises is whether policy should be introduced that would make the world look more like the competitive ideal? Would this make the world a better place?

Structure, conduct and performance

The idea of imperfect competition had been initially developed by writers such as Joan Robinson and Edward Chamberlin in the 1930s (as set out in Chapter 2). This led to the realisation that an industry could not only operate as if under perfect competition or as a monopoly. An industry (or a market) could follow a number of different models, depending on the characteristics of the market – in particular, the number of firms in the market, the way in which they interact and the existence of barriers to entry.

An influential book in this area was Joe Bain's *Industrial Organisation*, the first edition of which was published in 1959. He argued that the structure of a market would determine the way in which firms in the market conducted themselves, and that this in turn would determine the effectiveness of the performance of the market in allocating resources. This came to be known as the **structure–conduct–performance (SCP)** paradigm. The extent to which firms were free to enter a market, as opposed to facing barriers to entry, would be an important influence on market structure, and whether it would persist over time.

In the extreme position, a monopoly firm protected by strong barriers to entry would be able to restrict output and raise price, increasing its profits at the expense of consumers, and leaving society as a whole worse off. If firms in a market were able to collude together, they could act in the same way, which would also damage consumers.

This line of argument suggests that policy should be used in order to regulate the working of monopoly firms. Furthermore, a merger or acquisition that resulted in a more concentrated market would also merit investigation, if the result was a weakening of competition.

Legislation to combat monopolies is not new, but modern competition law developed from the Sherman Act of 1890 and the Clayton Act of 1914 in the USA. In the UK, most significant was the Monopolies and Restrictive Practices (Inquiry and Control) Act of 1948. Today, **competition policy** in the UK is the responsibility of the Competition and Markets Authority (CMA), which operates under the Competition Act of 1998, the Enterprise Act of 2002 and the Enterprise and Regulatory Reform Act of 2013. Where markets are seen to work at a European level, firms are also subject to European Union competition law. The CMA works to:

> promote competition for the benefit of consumers, both within and outside the UK. Our aim is to make markets work well for consumers, businesses and the economy.
>
> https://www.gov.uk/government/organisations/
> competition-and-markets-authority

This legislation is based on the idea that competition is good for the economy, and should be promoted. Consumers need to be protected from exploitation by firms.

Is monopoly always bad?

Joseph Schumpeter emphasised the importance of innovation in the process of economic change, for example in his 1942 book *Capitalism, Socialism and Democracy*. Invention and innovation would result in the appearance of monopoly firms, so that market structure changes in response to technological change. Such monopolies would be temporary as other firms caught up. In this context, the mere existence of a monopoly is not damaging for society – on the contrary it may contribute to economic growth.

It could also be argued that firms in a competitive environment would not be in a position to invest in research and development, whereas monopoly firms are able to use their profits to be innovative, and to improve the efficiency of production.

Furthermore, the mere existence of a monopoly or concentrated market does not necessarily mean that the firm or firms in the market will abuse their market position at the expense of consumers, especially if barriers to entry are weak. Indeed, if there are no barriers to the entry of new firms, the existing firms may choose not to exploit their position in order to avoid having to compete with new entrants.

Historically, the way in which legislation has been implemented in the USA and the UK has differed. In the USA, there has tended to be a presumption that monopoly is bad, whereas in the UK the approach has been to consider each market on its own merits, to see whether firms are abusing their market position.

There have been some high-profile cases in recent years. Perhaps the most famous was initiated in 1998, when Microsoft was accused of becoming a monopoly and abusing its market position in relation to PC operating systems and its web browser. Microsoft was also indicted under European legislation.

The organisation of firms

A further question is whether firms will always act to maximise profits. This may depend on the way in which a firm is organised internally. As a firm grows, its internal structure becomes more complex. There may come to be a separation between the owners of the firm (shareholders) and the managers responsible for day-to-day operational decisions. The managers are likely to have better information about the firm's operations than a fragmented set of shareholders, and may therefore not be fully accountable for their actions, allowing them to pursue their own interests. This is known as the **principal–agent problem**, and you will learn more about this during your studies.

Strategic interaction between firms

The use of game theory in economics has become widespread, especially being used to analyse the way in which firms will act strategically in a market in which there are relatively few firms operating. There are many ways in which firms may set out to out-think their rivals, or find ways of colluding to increase their joint profits without drawing the attention of the regulating authorities. This is an important way in which economists analyse whether a market will work in a way that favours or disadvantages consumers. It will almost certainly figure as part of your undergraduate degree programme.

Nationalisation and privatisation

Where an industry is characterised by substantial economies of scale relative to market demand, it is difficult for competition to be maintained, as the largest firm always has a cost advantage over smaller firms, and is able to dominate the market. This situation is known as a natural monopoly. If such industries are operated by profit-maximising firms, then this can create the very situation that anti-monopoly legislation is designed to prevent. However, forcing such firms to charge the competitive price would result in losses being made.

In the UK in the period immediately after the Second World War, a number of such industries were taken into public ownership, including electricity and gas supply, the railways, water supply, steel, coal and several others (not to mention the Bank of England). The Labour Party was especially keen to expand the role of the public sector in the economy. The taking of private industries or firms into public ownership is known as **nationalisation.**

By the 1980s, many of these industries were seen to be operating inefficiently. This was partly attributed to the principal–agent problem, in the sense that the managers of these nationalised industries were seen to be insufficiently accountable to their principals (the general public). When the Conservatives came to power under Margaret Thatcher with a renewed belief in the free market, there was a period of **privatisation**, with many of the nationalised industries and firms being transferred back into private ownership. A series of regulatory bodies (such as Ofwat and Ofgem) were set up in order to ensure that these enterprises attained productivity improvements and behaved responsibly by not exploiting their market power.

Market failure

During your undergraduate programme you will no doubt meet a variety of reasons why markets may fail to produce the desirable outcome for society. Without going into the technical detail, let's look at a couple of examples to give you a flavour of what is involved.

Asymmetric information

The principal–agent problem is one example of **asymmetric information**, a situation in which some partners to a transaction have different information from others. A famous example of this was set out by Nobel Laureate George Akerlof (1970) in *The Market for Lemons*.

This was not about citrus fruit, but about second-hand cars. We can think of cars as falling into two categories. There are good-quality cars that are reliable, fuel-efficient and comfortable. There are others that are for ever breaking down, that consume fuel excessively, and just seem more trouble than they are worth – US slang labels these as 'lemons'.

The problem arises if buyers cannot distinguish between 'good' cars and lemons – but, of course, the owner can. In other words, there is a situation of asymmetric information, as the seller has better information than potential buyers. Suppose the owner of a good car puts it on the market for what he or she sees as a good price, given that it is a 'good' car. A potential buyer will not be able to tell whether it is really good, or whether it is a lemon, so will want to offer a lower price to cover against the risk that it is a lemon. The seller will be reluctant to accept a lower offer, knowing it is a good car, and may thus choose not to sell.

Why does this matter? If all sellers of good cars act in the same way, then the market for good cars will fail, and only sellers of lemons will be able to sell.

There are other situations in which a similar argument applies. Health insurance is another possible example. Suppose someone with a recurrent health problem approaches an insurance company requesting insurance to cover hospital bills and other medical expenses. If the insurance company has no access to information about the applicant's health, it will need to impose a higher premium to cover the risk of having to pay out. It could then be that the only people who will take out health insurance will be those who know they will need to claim, whereas those in good health will find the cost of insurance unacceptable.

The solution to such situations is to find a way of improving the information available to both participants. A car dealer may offer a warranty on a car; the health insurer may require health checks on the person wanting insurance, or may issue terms of conditions that mean that they will not have to pay out for health issues that were present before the insurance contract was signed.

Pollution

Chapter 3 introduced the notion of an externality, where not all of the costs associated with an economic activity are reflected in the price of a transaction.

Pollution by a firm as part of its production activity is one example. If a firm emits toxic fumes as part of its production process, it imposes costs on society – and in particular on people living in the neighbourhood. If the firm does not have to meet these costs, then it will choose to produce a higher level of output (and hence higher levels of pollution) than is desirable from the perspective of the society.

It may be possible to correct for this market failure by imposing a tax on the firm, or by regulating the quantity of emissions. However, it may not always be straightforward to calculate the size of the tax needed, or the appropriate quantity used in regulation of emissions. One approach is to issue permits to pollute, and allow these to be traded between firms. The EU Emissions Trading System is an example of how this approach is being used to combat climate change, which operates across the 28 members of the EU plus Iceland, Liechtenstein and Norway.

The situation becomes even more complicated where the pollution crosses international borders, where it may be difficult to monitor the situation or to impose penalties for the pollution. For example, there have been occasions when airports in Singapore and Malaysia have had to close because of haze spreading from forest fires in neighbouring Indonesia. Furthermore, it may be difficult to reach agreement on whether the emission is indeed harmful – witness the debate around climate change, where some would deny that this is an issue at all.

Nobel Prize winner Ronald Coase highlighted the importance of trans-action costs and property rights in tackling this sort of issue. In the pollution example above, if the firm owns the right to pollute, it could be dissuaded from doing so if the local community offers to compensate it for using cleaner technology. Alternatively, if the local community owned the right to clean air, they could charge the firm for causing pollution.

References

Akerlof, G.A. (1970) The market for 'lemons': quality uncertainty and the market mechanism. *Quarterly Journal of Economics* 84(3):488–500.

Bain, J.S. (1959) *Industrial Organisation*. Chichester: Wiley.

Schumpeter, J.A. (1942, 2010) *Capitalism Socialism and Democracy*. Oxford: Routledge Classics.

5

Debates in macroeconomics and development

- discuss the evolution of macroeconomic thinking in the period since the Second World War
- highlight the links between developments in macroeconomic theory and macroeconomic performance
- explain how approaches to macroeconomic policy also evolved in response to unfolding events
- examine the growing gap between advanced and less-developed countries and the challenge of tackling global poverty
- show how approaches to promoting development in less-developed countries also evolved through time

The economics profession does not always get a good press. For example, many commentators seemed to take great pleasure in pointing out the failure of economists to predict the financial crisis that afflicted the global economy in the late 2000s.

Economists are notorious for disagreeing with each other. Common jokes about economists are:

- If you line up all the economists in the world, they will never reach a conclusion (this has been attributed to George Bernard Shaw).
- If you ask 10 economists a question you will get at least 11 different answers.

This is nowhere more apparent than in the way that economic theory and economic policy have evolved over the past 70 years. New theories lead to new approaches to policy, policy failure leads to new advances in theory, which lead to new approaches to policy – and so the cycle goes on.

This chapter explores how this process influenced theory and policy at the macroeconomic level, and looks at the consequences for less developed countries.

Revolution, counter-revolution and consensus in macroeconomics

The Keynesian Revolution had a major impact on macroeconomic thinking and on macroeconomic policy design in the post-war period. The introduction of the dollar standard system, under which countries pegged their exchange rates to the US dollar, meant that monetary policy could not be used for domestic stabilisation, as it had, for technical reasons, to be devoted to maintaining the value of the exchange rate. This gave prominence to the use of fiscal policy for stabilising the domestic economy, reinforcing the arguments put forward by Keynes.

Problems soon became apparent in the UK. During the 1950s and 1960s, if the government was tempted into stimulating the economy in order to achieve higher economic growth, the current account of the balance of payments was pushed into deficit because of an increase in imports. This then forced a period of austerity, so the UK economy went through a period of 'stop–go'.

A famous and influential article by the New Zealand economist Bill Phillips in 1958 claimed to have identified a relationship between the rate of unemployment and the rate of change of money wages. This appeared to have been a stable relationship over almost a hundred years in the UK. This implied that high unemployment would be associated with low unemployment, and vice versa. If this were indeed the case, a government knowing that an election was approaching could precipitate an increase in aggregate demand, leading to a fall in unemployment (hopefully with an increase in the popularity of the government). Inflation would also accelerate, but the effects of this would not be apparent until after the election, and the government could then deal with it by allowing unemployment to rise again. This was known as the **political business cycle**.

The escalation of the Vietnam War in the late 1960s added a new element. The USA funded the war partly by expanding the supply of money, which had a knock-on effect on other countries because of the operation of the dollar standard, and inflation began to accelerate in many countries. This contributed to the breakdown of the dollar standard, with many countries moving to a flexible exchange rate system in which the value of the currency was free to find its own level against other currencies.

One effect of this was to release monetary policy from its commitment to the exchange rate, allowing interest rates to be manipulated for domestic purposes. At the same time fiscal policy became less powerful.

It seemed that the effects of this were not fully understood, and when oil prices suddenly increased as a result of action by the OPEC cartel, the UK

Chancellor of the Exchequer tried to stave off an increase in unemployment by a monetary expansion, the result of which was the highest rate of inflation since 1917. You can see this in Figure 3.5.

The monetarist counter-revolution

At the time when inflation globally was accelerating in the late 1960s, Keynesian analysis came under attack from (Nobel Prize winner) Milton Friedman and others, who came to be known as the *monetarists*. Friedman became extremely influential, acting as a key advisor to Ronald Reagan in the USA and Margaret Thatcher in the UK during the 1980s.

The monetarists argued that the economy would return of its own accord to an equilibrium or 'natural' rate of unemployment, and that attempts to reduce unemployment below this rate would only result in inflation. This was essentially an updating of some ideas from Classical economics. These ideas were reinforced by the theory of *rational expectations*, which argued that economic agents would be well informed about the path of the economy, and would take actions that negated any attempts by government to alter the equilibrium position, which would be attained very quickly.

This belief that the free market would manage the aggregate economy implied that the most appropriate policy for a government to adopt would be neutral, controlling money supply in order to maintain a stable inflation rate. Other possible steps for the government would be to ensure that markets worked effectively, by introducing measures to improve the supply-side of the economy.

When oil prices rose again in 1979/80, the monetarist influence on policy became apparent. For example, look back at Figure 2.1, and check out the substantial rise in the unemployment rate that took place in the early 1980s, as the government resisted the temptation to stimulate aggregate demand. Other measures taken in this period involved reducing the power of trade unions to improve the flexibility of the labour market, and privatisation of nationalised industries and firms. These all reflect the belief that the free market would allow the macroeconomy to reach its natural equilibrium.

Inflation targeting and a move towards consensus

The Labour administration under Tony Blair that was elected in 1997 continued in similar style. The early policy of the new government included steps to enhance the credibility of government policy, and in particular a determination to maintain control over inflation. One of the first steps was to delegate the responsibility for monetary policy to the Bank of England, thus removing any possibility that the political business cycle would be invoked. The government set a target for the inflation rate, and the Bank of England was given independent responsibility to fix interest rates in order to achieve the target rate (currently set at 2% per annum). If at any time the inflation rate moved more than one percentage point away from the target rate (above or below), the Governor of the Bank would need to write an open letter to the Chancellor justifying the actions taken.

Governments elsewhere were taking similar action, and by the early 2000s the global economy (including that of the UK) was seen to be enjoying an unprecedented period of sustained economic growth and low inflation. In the face of this success, it seemed that macroeconomists had finally got things right, and reached some consensus about how the economy should be run.

But this could not last . . .

Cracks began to appear towards the end of the 2000s. Food prices accelerated, leading to an increase in inflation. During 2008, the inflation rate in the UK moved out of its target range, but the impact of this was dwarfed by the onset of a seemingly unexpected **financial crisis**. This began in the USA, but rapidly spread to other developed countries. In the UK, several banks found themselves struggling, and the authorities had to intervene to avoid their collapse. This effectively meant that banks in trouble were being nationalised, as they were seen to be 'too big to fail'.

Credit dried up, and aggregate demand fell. Recession set in. By early 2009, bank rate (the rate set by the Bank of England) was at an historic low of 0.5%, and could not be reduced further. The public sector's net debt increased substantially, partly but not entirely the result of bailing out the banks. This led for calls for austerity amidst fears that unemployment would rise.

Once again, macroeconomic thinking had to catch up with events, both to explain how this state of affairs had emerged and to find remedies.

It seemed that the focus of policy had been too much on ensuring that prices remained relatively stable, rather than on ensuring a secure flow of liquidity to the economy. With banks becoming ever more inventive in devising new ways of manipulating their balance sheets, lending had become more and more risky over time, creating a bubble that eventually burst.

Remedies included a device known as **quantitative easing**, whereby the Bank of England released more credit into the financial system, supported by improved regulation of the banks, the responsibility for which was again given to the Bank of England.

The UK economy recovered gradually from the recession under the new regime. Some other economies in the eurozone were less fortunate – in particular Greece, where an enormous public sector deficit forced a prolonged and deep recession.

These changes are still settling in, and you can look forward to exploring how things are developing during your studies, if you should choose to join an economics degree programme.

Poverty and development: the lost world

The final part of this chapter explores one of the greatest economic challenges facing the world today, a challenge that has been perplexing economists and policy-makers. This is the persistent and widening gap in living standards between the countries that have gone through a process of economic growth and development, and those that have remained less developed, characterised by low incomes and high levels of poverty. In particular, countries across sub-Saharan Africa have failed to make significant progress over several decades in spite of repeated efforts. Figure 5.1 shows something of the depth of the problem.

This shows levels of average incomes (measured by GNI per capita) in 2014 for a selection of countries around the globe – but with a focus on sub-Saharan Africa, where the problem is most severe. The contrast between the USA, with GNI per capita of around US$50,000, and Burundi (US$240) is stark. It should be noted that it is not only sub-Saharan Africa that faces this problem, as there are countries in other parts of the world that also remain less developed, for example in South Asia but also elsewhere.

After the Second World War, it seemed that the world was divided into three groups:

- the First World of capitalist market economies: countries in North America, Western Europe plus Japan;

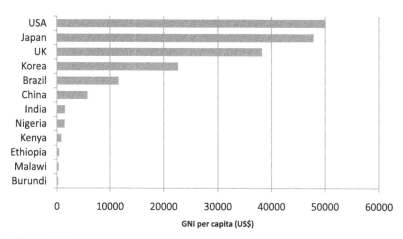

Figure 5.1 GNI per capita (US$) 2012, selected countries (*Source: Data from World Development Report 2014*).

- the Second World of the communist bloc: the USSR, Eastern Europe, China, etc.;
- the Third World: comprising all the rest.

The political scene was dominated by the Cold War between the West and the USSR, with the less-developed countries (LDCs) looking on.

Structural transformation

It is notable that no country has become developed without undergoing some sort of structural transformation, starting with the Industrial Revolution in Britain. Countries in sub-Saharan Africa are seen to continue to rely on low productivity agriculture or on mineral extraction.

The Classical economists had believed that the presence of diminishing returns in the agricultural sector would mean that markets for labour would always tend towards some subsistence wage, rather than being able to experience economic growth. If average incomes began to increase, population growth would exceed output growth and average incomes would fall back.

Nobel Laureate Sir Arthur Lewis published what was to become an influential article in 1954. He argued that the traditional (primarily agricultural) sector in a less developed economy would be characterised by surplus labour, in the sense that if workers were withdrawn from the sector, this would have no discernible effect on output. For example, it might be that a farm is run by the members of a household, dividing up the work between them. It could well be that there is not really enough work to occupy all members of the household fully, so that some of them could be withdrawn without affecting the quantity of output produced.

If such surplus labour is widespread, an economy could develop by having the wage in the capitalist (industrial) sector set at a level that would attract labour to migrate, allowing an increase in output. This would then lead to self-sustaining economic growth as the industrial surplus was reinvested. This approach emphasises industry as being the driving force for economic growth, and led to the view that industrialisation was the way forward for countries wanting to achieve development. Unfortunately, in some cases this led to the neglect of agriculture, which stagnated, whilst industries too often failed to take off.

Economic growth

How should industrialisation and economic growth be achieved? Sir Roy Harrod in the UK and Evsey Domar in the USA, working independently, built on Keynesian ideas, looking at how equilibrium in a Keynesian world would be maintained under conditions of economic growth. Their work came to be known as the *Harrod–Domar* model, which argued that the viable economic growth rate for an economy depended on the rate of savings and the efficiency of capital.

Policy-makers saw this approach as emphasising the importance of savings to generate growth. Savings would enable investment, which would allow physical capital to expand, raising the productive capacity of the economy and resulting in an increase in incomes, which would then feed back into higher savings. For example, this was built into India's Five-Year Plans, which aimed to increase savings in order to foster economic growth.

Another Nobel Laureate, Robert Solow, switched the focus away from savings behaviour, focusing on the importance of technological progress for enabling long-term economic growth. An increase in the saving rate would provide a one-off increase in average income, but only improvements in productivity would result in an increase in the long-run growth rate. Importantly, such gains can be achieved not only by using better capital equipment, but also by improving the quality of labour, through education and training.

Spending on improved health care, education and training can be seen as a form of investment in **human capital**. Human capital is the stock of skills, expertise and physical qualities that contribute to a worker's productivity.

Changing perspectives

To some extent, the approach to promoting development in LDCs mirrored the changes in macroeconomic theory and policy that were taking place in the advanced capitalist economies. This in part arose from the influence of the IMF and the World Bank.

In the Keynesian period after the war, aid provided by the USA enabled Europe to reconstruct its infrastructure. The success of this led to the view that overseas assistance for LDCs could provide the injection of finance needed to initiate a process of economic growth. However, this has not been as effective as had been hoped.

An important debate at this time was whether a country should go all out for growth in the expectation that the effects would spread through the society, or whether a country should first put resources into dealing with the basic needs of the population, so that people would then be better fitted to be productive members of society.

The collapse of the dollar standard and the first oil price crisis in 1973/74 created a new set of problems. LDCs with no oil reserves suddenly found themselves facing severe deficits on their balance of payments. At this time, the IMF would only provide loans for countries in difficulties on condition that they imposed austerity on their economies. For LDCs this was punishing, and many of them borrowed on international financial markets in order to cope, often under flexible interest rate terms.

When the second oil price hike occurred in 1989/90, macroeconomic thinking had changed with the monetarist counter-revolution, and many developed economies were adopting monetarist policies, increasing interest rates in order to stabilise their economies. For the LDCs facing debt repayments on variable-interest loans, this was disastrous. Measures taken in order to safeguard the international financial system focused on rescheduling debt repayments, leaving LDCs with unsustainable debts that had been postponed into the future.

John Williamson (1990) set out 10 policies that became known as the **Washington Consensus**, which were intended to capture the approach being adopted as advice recommended by the IMF and World Bank. These were all based on the conventional wisdom of the time – that market forces would be effective in allocating resources if only governments would allow them to do so. A government should only intervene if markets fail to work. This is captured in the following extract from the World Bank's *World Development Report 1991*:

> Put simply, governments need to do less in those areas where markets work, or can be made to work reasonably well . . . at the same time governments need to do more in those areas where markets alone cannot be relied upon.

The package of policies included encouragement for LDCs to open themselves up to more international trade, and to accept foreign direct investment from multinational corporations, together with deregulating domestic markets and reducing the role of the State.

Globalisation

This was also a period in which a process of globalisation was taking place, defined by Joseph Stiglitz (2002) as:

> Fundamentally, [globalisation] is the closer integration of countries and peoples of the world which has been brought about by the enormous reduction of costs of transportation and communication, and the breaking down of artificial barriers to the flows of goods, services, capital, knowledge, and (to a lesser extent) people across borders.

Transport and communications worldwide had been revolutionised by technological advance, and this combined with deregulation of markets to create a much more interconnected world. Critics have argued that LDCs suffered from this, being unprepared for the impact of the competitive forces that they faced in the global arena, especially from multinational corporations.

As time went by, it was all too apparent that the Washington Consensus was not achieving the objective of encouraging development and alleviating poverty. A key factor that was holding LDCs back was the unsustainable debt levels facing many poor countries. Repayment of debt was consuming resources that could have been used to create development opportunities and alleviate poverty. Many people argued that if LDCs were not going to be able to pay the debt, it would make more sense to forgive the debt altogether. However, it was argued that if this were to happen, countries would believe that they would always get away with getting into debt, and thus start all over again with borrowing and squandering.

The World Bank and IMF launched the Heavily Indebted Poor Countries Initiative (HIPC), which would provide debt forgiveness to countries that could demonstrate a commitment to following approved policies and committing resources to the alleviation of poverty. The conditions imposed were so stringent that few countries seemed likely to be able to comply, and in response to pressure groups the HIPC conditions were relaxed in 1999.

Several reasons have been put forward to explain the failure of the Washington Consensus policies. These include weak governance in many LDCs, with corruption being an issue in some. It was also argued that more clearly targeted poverty reduction policies were needed to ensure that all citizens benefited from growth.

The Millennium Development Goals

At the United Nations Millennium Summit held in 2000, 149 world leaders committed their nations to a new global partnership to reduce extreme poverty. Specific targets were set for eight key **Millennium Development Goals (MDGs)**, to:

- eradicate extreme poverty and hunger
- achieve universal primary education
- promote gender equality and empower women
- reduce child mortality
- improve maternal health
- combat HIV/AIDS, malaria and other diseases
- ensure environmental sustainability
- develop a global partnership for development.

  http://www.un.org/en/events/pastevents/millennium_summit.shtml

These targets (which were specific for each country) were to be achieved by 2015. In 2015, the UN described this scheme as having been 'the most successful anti-poverty movement in history . . .' Success in reaching the targets varied between regions, with sub-Saharan Africa in particular falling short in some key areas.

A new sustainable development agenda and a new global agreement on climate change were developed to build on the success of the MDGs. At the United Nations Sustainable Development Summit in September 2015, world leaders adopted the 2030 Agenda for Sustainable Development, which includes 'a set of 17 Sustainable Development Goals (SDGs) to end poverty, fight inequality and injustice and tackle climate change by 2030' (http://www.undp.org/content/undp/en/home/mdgoverview/post-2015-development-agenda.html).

The SDGs are also known as the 'Global Goals'.

References

Lewis, W.A. (1954) Economic development with unlimited supplies of labour. *The Manchester School* 22:139–191.

Stiglitz, J. (2002) *Globalization and its Discontents*. London: Allen Lane.

Williamson, J. (1990) 'What Washington means by policy reform', in Williamson, J. (ed.) *Stabilization and Reforms in Latin America: Where Do We Stand?* Frankfurt: Vervuert.

6

Economics as a science?

- discuss the status of economics as a social science
- comment on whether economics or any other discipline that sets out to explain human behaviour can be described as a science
- explore how economics uses scientific method as a non-experimental science, in particular by calling on mathematics and statistical analysis
- note the increasing use of experimental methods to explore economic hypotheses
- identify the flexibility of economics degree programmes and the possibilities for combining the study of economics with that of other subjects

Physics is a 'science'. History is an 'arts' subject that is part of 'humanities'. Music is a creative art. But how do we classify economics?

And does it matter?

This chapter discusses the approach that is adopted in undertaking economic analysis. It will also explore why it is that economists often seem unable to forecast what is about to happen in the economy, and looks at the ways in which economics interacts with and draws upon other disciplinary approaches.

The economics approach

We like to be able to categorise things, to put things in compartments. When it comes to thinking about economics, for some reason, people like to be able to say whether or not it is a science. It has never been clear to me why this matters. If you look at the range of undergraduate programmes in economics that are offered by universities in the UK, you will find that the titles of the awards vary. Some will offer a Bachelor of Arts (BA), whereas others may offer a Bachelor of Science (BSc). Some offer a BSc (Econ), or even a Bachelor of Science in the Social Sciences (BSc (SocSci)).

Does this mean that universities cannot decide whether or not economics can be classified as a science or not? Not necessarily. It may depend on historical accident, or on the administrative structure of a university. Some universities may offer a mixture of award titles, depending on whether and how economics is combined with other subjects. We will come back to this later.

In the discussions about whether or not economics is a science, there are two standout issues that arise: the nature of the *subject matter* of economic analysis and the *approach* that is adopted by the discipline.

The subject matter of economics

Economics deals with aspects of society, which entails seeking to explain decisions taken by people in the context of their social interactions, by firms operating in a changeable environment, and by governments swayed by political considerations.

This raises questions about whether any academic discipline that studies human behaviour can be classified as a 'science'. Given that individuals differ from each other because of their diverse characteristics, can we ever expect them to behave consistently? Indeed, some individuals may behave differently on different days depending on their mood, or on the weather. Of course, this would also apply to other disciplines such as sociology – but with economics there is perhaps more of an obsession with deciding if it is a science. The compromise solution is to define an intermediate category of disciplines known as the *social sciences*.

Economics and the scientific method

An argument that is put forward to justify economics being classified as a science is that it uses 'scientific method'. In other words, could we claim that economics displays the sort of rigour expected in science, at least in terms of the methods that it employs?

There are many ways of describing 'the scientific method', but a typical sequence is set out in Figure 6.1.

The approach begins with *observation* – a researcher observes something that seems worthy of investigation. This would lead to a research *question* that captures a key item of interest arising from the observation. From the question, a *testable hypothesis* is devised that provides a possible explanation of or answer to the question. The next phase is to design and carry out an *experiment* that will provide evidence for testing the hypothesis. Analysing the

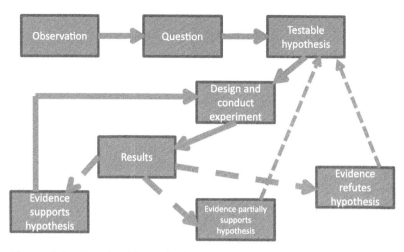

Figure 6.1 The scientific method.

results of the experiment then allows one of three possible conclusions to be drawn.

One possibility is that the evidence from the experiment supports the hypothesis, in which case the experiment should be repeated or refined in order to allow evidence to accumulate in favour of the hypothesis. If the evidence only partially supports the hypothesis, or if the evidence turns out to be inconsistent with the hypothesis, then the hypothesis needs to be revised or refined. At this stage it may be that an entirely new hypothesis needs to be developed, and a new experiment carried out.

How well does economics measure up to this method? The general approach would be widely accepted. Economists observe aspects of the economy and economic decisions being made. They formulate a research question, and from that would identify an appropriate hypothesis to be tested. They would then set out to test that hypothesis, drawing on mathematical or statistical methods. Based on the results they would then evaluate the strength of the evidence to see whether it supported or rejected the hypothesis.

If you re-read that last paragraph, you will see that there is one key word that is missing – namely 'experiment'. Although there is an increasing body of economics research that relies on undertaking experiments, it is more common to find economists relying on mathematical and statistical techniques when setting out to test hypotheses about economic behaviour.

It is also noticeable that there are very few *laws* in economics that are universally accepted as having been proved. In many areas of economics, it is not possible to prove a theory, in the sense that it will always be applicable in all circumstances. The best to be hoped is that evidence will continue to accumulate in favour of a hypothesis. However, it is possible to reject a theory on the grounds that it is not supported by the evidence.

Why is this? It is partly because of the complexity of the economy, and the way that economic variables interact with each other. No matter how comprehensive an economic model is designed to be, it is always possible that some new influence will turn up tomorrow, and turn everything on its head. It also comes back to the point made earlier, that we are dealing with human behaviour. People may behave differently tomorrow, so tomorrow's evidence may alter the conclusions. However, this is painting too gloomy a picture, as there are aspects of behaviour that are not subject to such variation.

Economics as a non-experimental discipline

How does economics manage to follow the scientific method given the difficulty of designing and conducting experiments?

Economics is not primarily a laboratory science (although there is a growing interest in experimentation, as we will see shortly). It cannot introduce policy changes just in order to see what happens. For example, it would not be politically acceptable to eliminate all social security payments to see what happens to poverty in the country!

Economics is not alone in this inability to undertake experiments. Meteorology is one example, where it is not possible to induce changes in climatic conditions in order to test hypotheses about climate change. Evolutionary biologists cannot accelerate the process of evolution in order to test their theories about the survival of the fittest. Only the development of the Large Hadron Collider (at enormous expense) has allowed astrophysicists to test hypotheses about the inter-relationship between quantum mechanics and general relativity.

This issue is common across the social sciences, where hypotheses and theories are put to the test through a range of approaches: conducting surveys, observing behaviour or analysing data.

In economics, two important approaches are through mathematical modelling and the analysis of statistical data.

Mathematical modelling

Chapter 1 explained that economists attempt to understand the world by building models of reality that enable them to focus on key economic relationships. What do these models look like?

There are times when a model can be represented in a simple diagram. An example of this was presented in Chapter 3, when the demand and supply model was introduced. Diagrams can take the analysis some distance, but are inevitably limited, as they are drawn in a two-dimensional space, when we often need to deal with much more complex interrelationships.

Mathematics offers a more flexible approach. This entails expressing the assumptions that underpin a model of economic behaviour as mathematical equations. These can then be manipulated using algebraic techniques to see the logical implications of those assumptions. These can then be compared with the reality of how economic agents behave in practice. This approach will be explored in Chapter 8.

Econometrics

A second approach is to take advantage of the increasing amount of data that is available about economic behaviour. For example, the Office for National Statistics publishes a wide range of data about the economy, some of which covers a relatively long period of time – this is known as time-series data. This covers things like GNI and its components, prices, unemployment and so on. There may also be cross-section data, observations of the same economic variable across different locations or across households.

Some university economics departments have invested in facilities in the form of Bloomberg terminals identical to those used in city trading. This not only allows you to become familiar with the software used by financial professionals, but also gives you access to data that can form the basis of your research project. Universities also provide you with top-class computing facilities and databases, such as that of the World Bank.

Econometrics is the application of mathematical and statistical techniques to economic data in order to test economic hypotheses and theories. A key aspect of this approach is the need to be able to express economic hypotheses in a form that allows the data to be used for testing purposes.

It is important to realise that it is not sufficient to discover an association or *correlation* between two variables. This of itself does not prove that there is a cause-and-effect relationship between them. For example, the fact that two variables move together through time does not necessarily mean that there is a causal linkage between them. It could just be that they are both related to some other unidentified variable. For example, a well-known example is that both ice-cream sales and the murder rate increase during the summer period. This does not mean that a ban on selling ice cream would result in fewer murders! Or that more rigorous policing would damage the sale of ice cream. Instead there may be a common factor that affects both – hot weather, perhaps.

This is where the scientific method approach to econometric analysis becomes important: it is part of a process to test hypotheses, not a question of looking for random associations between variables, and then looking for a theory that fits the facts. This sort of reasoning is likely to be part of your economics education. In addition there are econometric techniques that can shed light on the direction of causality between economic variables, so we can see which determines which.

It is also important to be aware that statistical analysis is only ever as good as the data that are used as inputs. If the data have not been accurately observed in the first place, then little reliance can be placed on the results – and economic variables are notoriously difficult to measure with accuracy. Nonetheless, this is an important way in which economists try to test their economic analysis against empirical reality.

Economics as an experimental discipline

Although neoclassical economics focused on rational economic decision-making, this approach has come under increasing criticism in recent years, and there is a growing interest in new ways of understanding and observing human economic behaviour. Some of this work draws on experimental methods used in psychology, and there is much scope for bringing economists and psychologists to work together in this area.

Laboratory experiments have been used to explore such issues as whether consumers do indeed act to maximise utility, or whether they may sometimes act in ways that might be construed as being non-rational. For example, do individuals act from purely altruistic motives on occasion, rather than purely aiming to maximise their own utility? Or perhaps they sometimes act with an awareness of social responsibility? Experiments can also explore the incentives that cause people to take economic decisions in a particular way, and to gauge how people react to conditions of risk and uncertainty.

A number of universities now have laboratories that allow experiments to be run under controlled conditions. It is possible that you will have the opportunity to be a participant in an economics experiment during your degree programme – or even to conduct an experiment yourself. The advances in computer technology and the internet have expanded the opportunities for this style of research.

Some of these experiments take the form of economic games, some of which are designed for use in the lecture theatre. You may well meet some of these, which are intended to get you thinking about economic processes, the way in which individuals reach decisions or make deals, and the way that these come together in a marketplace.

A rather different experimental approach has been borrowed from medical research. In testing new drugs, it is common practice to evaluate a drug or treatment with reference to a group of patients, some of whom will be given the drug to be tested, while the rest are given a placebo. The evaluation is then undertaken by analysing the differing reactions of the two groups.

In economic analysis, this approach can be used, through a process known as a randomised trial. As an example, suppose the government of a less-developed country wants to evaluate an anti-poverty policy, in which families are given financial support on condition that they send their children to school.

In order to test whether this will be effective in alleviating poverty, the government chooses a selection of villages that are similar in terms of size, composition and poverty level. It then implements the policy in some of the villages but not in the others. It can then observe any differences between the villages that have received the 'treatment' and those that did not. In some cases, this sort of situation may arise because a policy has been implemented in one place and not another, creating a form of natural experiment.

Economics and other disciplinary approaches

It has been noted that some parts of economics are now drawing on psychology for inspiration for some of its research. As you consider whether studying economics is for you, you may think that you would prefer to keep your options open by studying economics alongside another subject. This not only gives you exposure to the way that economists think and work, but also provides insights into alternative approaches.

There are plenty of opportunities for you to put this into effect, as there are many undergraduate programmes on offer in higher education (HE) institutions. You can browse these on the Unistats website (https://unistats.direct.gov. uk/find-out-more/key-information-set), which provides a Key Information Set (KIS) for every undergraduate programme on offer. The information is provided in a common framework, and every UK HE institution is required to supply this information for each of its undergraduate programmes – and to do so accurately.

The KIS data set lists more than 700 undergraduate programmes in the UK that include the word 'economics' in the title, from about 100 institutions. Sixty-nine institutions offer what are known as 'single honours' programmes, in which you specialise in 'economics', either just called economics, or programmes in some of the branches of economics, such as Applied Economics, Business (or Management) Economics, International Development, Financial Economics, Industrial Economics, International Economics or Mathematical Economics.

These programmes allow you to develop your knowledge of economics in some depth, although there may be opportunities to glimpse other subjects to some extent. If you have ambitions to study economics beyond the undergraduate level, perhaps to proceed to postgraduate study or economics research or to become a professional economist, then you will probably want to consider these single honours programmes.

Many universities also offer so-called 'joint' degrees, in which you would divide your time between two main subjects. The KIS data set lists almost 80 different subjects that can be combined with economics in this way. We will look at the most popular combinations below. In these programmes, the split of your study time between the two subjects would be approximately equal.

The advantage is to give you different perspectives on economic issues, and to provide insight into the way that different subject specialists approach ideas and think in different ways.

An increasing trend in recent years has been for some universities to offer a flexible structure that allows you to 'major' in one subject, but to follow another discipline in a 'minor' part of your study. Under these schemes, you would spend perhaps three-quarters of your time on your major subject, and a quarter on your minor. This means that you have sufficient time to study your main subject in some depth, but also get a coherent introduction to a second discipline.

If you have never studied economics before, and are considering taking up a degree course in the subject – but are not sure whether it is for you, then look for a programme that would allow you to embark on a single or joint honours programme, but with the option of switching at the end of the first year, once you have discovered more about the subject. (But keep reading this book, which will offer more advice about what to expect!)

Although there are about 80 different subjects that can be followed as a joint degree with economics, some of these are only offered by one or two institutions, and may perhaps be considered as minority interest subjects to study alongside economics, such as Egyptology, Astrophysics, Neuroscience or Latin. However, here are some of the more popular combinations on offer.

Economics and business (or management) (55 institutions)

Business (or management) is the most common offering as a joint degree with economics. This is perhaps not surprising as the connections between these subjects are fairly obvious. Business and management as subjects focus more on types and aspects of organisations, and the way that companies operate. Economics takes a rather different approach, although there is an overlap between industrial economics and parts of business and management studies.

One peculiarity of UK universities is that there is no consistency about where economics as a discipline is located in terms of the administrative structure of the institution. In some cases, economics is seen as part of the Business or Management School, sitting alongside departments of business, management, management science, accounting or finance. In other cases, economics is seen as part of social sciences, thus sitting alongside politics, international relations and sociology or social policy.

Does this matter? Not necessarily. The nature of the economics group will reflect the pattern of their research interests. An economics department that is located in social sciences may have a more varied research portfolio, whereas in the business school there may be a greater focus on the theory of the firm. However, this is by no means a general rule, and when you start to decide on your programme, you should visit the website of the economics group and see where their interests lie, as this may affect the nature and content of the programmes that they run – regardless of where they sit in the university.

Economics and finance (41 institutions)

As a subject, finance differs from business and management in its focus on investment and finance. Finance addresses the ways in which money is raised and distributed, looking at the measurement and management of risk, the role of financial assets and the operation of capital markets.

The recent financial crisis had very public and obvious effects on the 'real' economy, and the interaction between economics and finance has become an important topic for debate. In this context, it seems more important than ever that economists have an appreciation of the importance of the financial sector for the economy.

Economics and accounting (25 institutions)

The accountancy profession is an attractive option for many, and degree programmes that offer exemptions from some of the professional examinations that need to be passed for entering the profession continue to be popular.

Accounting and economics offer quite different academic approaches, but the two subjects are not so far apart that there is nothing to be gained from studying them in tandem.

Closely allied with accounting is actuarial science, which can be studied at 11 UK institutions according to the KIS. However, there is only one institution that offers actuarial science as a combination with economics.

Economics and politics (or international relations) (51 institutions)

The second most popular combination combines economics with the study of politics or international relations. Again, this is understandable in terms of the connections that exist between the subject matter of these disciplines. In particular, the synergies come in terms of the design and operation of policies and the impact of political factors on economic decisions.

If you are interested in the way in which governments work, and the way in which policy is formulated, then this combination will be an attractive option for you.

Economics and philosophy (18 institutions)

As has been discussed in earlier chapters, economics as a discipline evolved partly from the writing of the philosophers of early generations, but the links between the two subjects continue to attract students into joint study.

The more obvious connection between the subjects comes through the history of economic thought, but a bonus is that philosophers offer a way of thinking about issues that complements the economists' approach. A graduate who has studied these two subjects will have valuable skills in being able to approach problem solving from different perspectives.

Philosophy, politics and economics (27 institutions)

This traditional combination of three subjects has always been a popular one. Indeed, many of today's leading politicians and public figure studied PPE, which provides a broad understanding of the three disciplinary approaches and the insights provided by each.

In some cases, you may find it is possible to start on a PPE programme, but then decide to specialise in one or two of them after the first year. If your prime interest is in economics, you may find that the depth of study will be less than in a full economics programme, but if your aim is to enter politics, this may be a good option.

Economics and mathematics (37 institutions)

Mathematics as a partner for economics is a popular choice. Of course, this partly reflects the importance of mathematics as a tool used by economists. Indeed, some may regard much economic analysis as being a form of applied mathematics, so it is natural to see them as partners in study.

This combination can work well for many students, as economists need mathematical skills, but mathematicians benefit from having to present ideas in verbal style, as they must do if they are to be successful in economics. If you enjoy maths but want to broaden your horizons a little, this combination could be good for you.

Economics and a language (26 institutions)

Many UK institutions offer a programme that pairs study of economics with study of a language – indeed, there are at least 24 different languages that I came across in the KIS data set. Many of these programmes include a year spent studying in the foreign country.

In an increasingly globalised world, where there is so much movement of people and speedy transport and communication links around the world, the potential value of studying economics in combination with a language is clear.

If you have some facility with languages and think that you might work abroad at some point in the future, a joint degree studying economics alongside a language could bring rewards in the future. Studying abroad will broaden your mind and give you many advantages.

Economics and history (21 institutions)

This is another subject pairing that is offered by a significant number of institutions. In some cases, the combination is specifically with economic history, which offers an obvious synergy between the two disciplines. The ways in which historical developments in the economy have affected economic theory have been discussed in earlier chapters. Furthermore, there is a feedback from developments in economic analysis to affect the way in which societies have developed.

Economics and law (14 institutions)

The economy operates within a legal framework, and the law governs the way in which firms and markets work. The links between economics and law can thus offer some interesting interactions, and the two disciplines have different but complementary approaches to problem solving and analysis.

Economics and geography (13 institutions)

Human geography deals with locational issues, but also overlaps with economics in many ways. How did the location of industry come to be the way it is? Why does unemployment vary between regions in the way that it does? Are these economic or geographic issues? Economic geography has become an important part of the discipline, so again, the synergies with economics are apparent.

Economics and psychology (five institutions)

Having talked earlier in the chapter about the growing interaction between recent developments in economic analysis and aspects of psychology, it is surprising to find from the KIS data set that there are only five institutions in the UK that offer Economics and Psychology as a subject pairing – and all of these are in Scotland.

There is a lot of scope for economists who are familiar with aspects of psychology, and it is a shame that the options for studying the two together are so limited. Perhaps that will change as behavioural economics becomes more important.

Other pairings

There are many other subjects that can be partnered with economics for undergraduate study, and if there is a particular combination that interests you, then you should browse the KIS data set.

7

Economics and society

This chapter will:

- discuss how economics helps to shape policies designed and implemented by government
- identify different approaches adopted by centrally planned and market-oriented societies
- explore how economics can play a significant role in meeting some of the key challenges facing individual nations and the global economy
- comment on some of the branches of economics that are likely to feature in your degree programme

If economics is a *social* science, how does it help us to understand how society works?

A first point to notice is that the design and implementation of economic policy, whether at the microeconomic or macroeconomic level, is a major influence on economic *and* social behaviour. Economic policy is an important route through which government affects the way in which people behave, and by which it fulfils its mandate and expresses its ideology. This is the case whether the society is governed by democracy or through central planning or dictatorship. Furthermore, economics and economists have an important contribution to provide to the public debate on the key issues facing nations and the world as a whole.

This chapter explores the relationship between government and policy and explores the role of economics in seeking solutions for some major issues. It also introduces you to some of the options that may be available to you when studying economics at university, highlighting some of the sub-disciplines of economics that focus on particular areas of discussion and analysis.

Government and policy

In a democratic society, the elected government receives a mandate from the voters to pursue the set of objectives set out in its manifesto. It can be held to account by the voters in the next election. This may be seen as an example of the principal–agent problem, where the government acts as the agent of the voters (the principals). The 2010 election failed to produce a clear-cut result for a single party, and resulted in the formation of a coalition. As a result, neither of the parties in the coalition could fully realise their manifesto commitments, and the collapse of the Liberal Democrat vote in 2015 may have partly reflected the voters' wish to hold their party to account, although of course there are many other possible interpretations.

A significant component of the manifestos of the parties is economic in nature. For example, the manifestos set out different views about the relative desirable size of the public and private sectors. In other words, to what extent should the government intervene in the economy rather than leaving the market mechanism to allocate resources? In general terms, parties on the 'left' tend to favour more intervention, in particular in relation to social security. Parties on the 'right' tend to prefer a more market-based approach.

The differences across the political spectrum can partly be interpreted in terms of differing views about market failure. For example, how well can markets operate in the provision of education (including higher education) or health care? To what extent should the government intervene to influence the distribution of resources between groups in society in order to protect the poor and vulnerable?

In a dictatorship or under a system of central planning, the government takes decisions more directly on behalf of the people, but arguably the level of accountability to the people is weaker.

The experience of post-Revolution Russia in the interwar years offers one example. Resources were directed into the development of heavy industry at the expense of consumption, causing poverty and deprivation, but yet allowing the economy to develop. The price mechanism was used as a tool by the ruling regime as one way of providing incentives for firms to produce what was required in the view of the authorities. However, the logistics of micro-managing the economy produced some unhelpful results at times. For example, in the absence of a market price system, how does the State ensure that firms produce the nails that society needs? In practice, firms were given quotas instructing them how much output of nails was required. In some cases, they were given a quota expressed as the number of nails needed; in other instances the quota was expressed in terms of weight. This provided some bizarre incentives: in the former case, firms faced the incentive to produce large numbers of small nails, whereas in the latter situation, firms produced a very small number of very big (i.e. heavy) nails.

In contrast, the island state of Singapore was governed in a one-party system under Lee Kuan Yew, who was prime minister from 1957 until 1990. In this case, markets were enabled to operate effectively, transforming the country into a developed high-income society. There was intervention in many areas of the economy, but this complemented the market mechanism rather than attempting to substitute for it.

The nature of institutions can have a significant impact on the long-term development of an economy. In a stable political environment, the ruling authorities face incentives to implement policies that encourage long-run improvements in living conditions. However, if the government does not expect to survive into the future, and lacks the sense of accountability to its populace, the incentive is to make the most of the present and adopt short-termist policies. Why use available funds for projects that will not deliver benefit until some uncertain time in the future, when short-run measures will deliver apparent gains now – or when funds can be diverted for personal gain?

Important decisions taken by government relate to the timing of expenditures and borrowing. To what extent should resources be used to improve living conditions for future generations at the expense of the current population? Or to what extent should today's population enjoy consuming goods if this depletes resources available to future generations? In other words, the *sustainability* of economic growth needs to be considered.

Economic analysis provides the means by which government can implement its policies. In doing so, economics provides *positive*, rather than *normative* guidance. In other words (as explained in Chapter 1), economics sets out how a particular policy is likely to work, but without making a value judgement on whether that policy should be used. This is not to say that economists do not have views, but that they can also take an objective approach to the analysis of the likely effects of implementing a particular policy.

Meeting challenges

Looking around, it is clear that we live in an imperfect world. There are many areas in which economists can contribute significantly to the debates on the challenges facing individual countries and the global community. If you choose to study economics at university, you will find out about some or all of these challenges and get to understand how economics is relevant in tackling them. In this section, we introduce some of these topics – but it is in no way a comprehensive list.

Environmental sustainability

Can economic growth be sustainable over the long term? This has been a debating point over many years. Back in 1987, the Brundtland Commission defined **sustainable development** as 'development which meets the needs of the present without compromising the ability of future generations to meet their own needs' (WCED, 1987, p. 4). This oft-quoted definition echoes the discussion of the previous section about the need to balance the concern for today's generation with that of the future.

One aspect of this is climate change, whereby the planet is gradually warming up due to the build-up of greenhouse gas emissions, with major consequences for the future of the planet. There has been much debate about the causes of this (or even the validity of it), and about how the world community can respond to it. The debate has been influenced by the lobbying of various pressure groups with different interests – oil companies, 'green' campaigners, less-developed countries, and so on.

Economists have an important role to play in understanding how the situation has arisen, and in framing policies that may be able to tackle the problem, or at least alleviate its effects. The *Stern Review on the Economics of Climate Change* is the most well-known and most widely discussed report highlighting the issues surrounding climate change. The 700-page report was authored by the economist Lord Stern.

In particular, the economic analysis of externalities casts some light on the mechanisms in the free market that lead to pollution at a level that is damaging to society. Economics can also be invoked to evaluate alternative policies that could be used to alter incentives faced by economic agents in order to reduce emissions, including policies to tax or regulate. The pollution permit approach to the problem is also based upon economic analysis.

Further insights come from analysing the characteristics of non-renewable resources and the extent to the rate of depletion depends upon market incentives. This is part of a piece of analysis known as the *Tragedy of the Commons*, which explores how goods with certain characteristics are liable to be over-consumed. For example, this helps us to understand how over-fishing can lead to the extinction of species. The tragedy of the commons was not first popularised by an economist, but by the ecologist Garrett Harbin (although it had earlier been outlined by William Forster Lloyd, who wrote on economics in the early nineteenth century). However, economic analysis provides important insights to its significance, and in 2009 Elinor Ostrom became the first woman to be awarded the Nobel Prize in Economic Sciences for her work on economic governance, especially in relation to governing the commons.

The nation's health

It is now well established that smoking tobacco is damaging to health – and that people who smoke demonstrate extreme reluctance to take this into account. It is also apparent that in spite of warnings, young people continue to take up smoking, only to find that they cannot give it up.

Policies to discourage people from smoking tobacco have been based on economic analysis. Initially, it was hoped that imposing taxes would help, but it emerged that demand was highly inelastic, so that even relatively large taxes had little impact. The next step was to identify that another possible remedy was to address the information failure – on the assumption that if people did not fully comprehend the damage to health from smoking, then providing information and warnings would assist in discouraging people. When this also proved insufficient, the use of direct regulation was the next step, through prohibiting smoking in public buildings. At each stage of this, economic analysis provided guidance.

Economic analysis also figures in the evaluation of new treatments for medical conditions. This has been a contentious issue on a number of recent occasions, as the allocation of scarce resources in the NHS forces difficult choices to be made. There have been situations in which individuals have requested access to experimental (and expensive) treatments, without which they would not survive. Given that resources are scarce, should these demands be met at the expense of limiting the resources used for treatments that could save greater numbers of people? The notion of opportunity cost is central to this debate, and the economic tool of **benefit–cost analysis** becomes important in coming to a reasoned decision. Benefit–cost (or cost–benefit) analysis is a technique that involves balancing the benefits of a project over its lifetime against its costs, taking into account externalities and recognising it is important to balance future benefits against present costs in a consistent manner.

Project evaluation

Benefit–cost analysis also plays a role when it comes to taking decisions on large-scale investment projects aimed at improving the country's infrastructure. An example is the high-speed rail project (HS2). Such projects require thorough investigation of all the benefits and costs, covering not only the direct benefits (such as shorter journey times) and costs (new rails to be laid), but also the indirect benefits and costs – the externalities involved through the effects on the environment and the impact on alternative modes of transport. Economists have developed ways of quantifying the benefits and costs, and of taking into account the key issue that many of the costs come in the short run, whereas the benefits come in the long run. HS2 is just one example, of course.

The analysis is also used for other large-scale projects (such as the mounting of the London Olympics). The approach is by no means perfect, as it rests on assumptions and forecasts. However, it does offer a way of comparing alternative projects, and thus evaluating the opportunity cost of one project relative to another.

Crisis and recession

In the wake of the financial crisis of the late 2000s and the subsequent global recession, economics came under a lot of criticism about its failure to have predicted what was to occur. This can in part be attributed to the nature of economic analysis, in the sense that models that are built on assumptions that reflect past reality may not be able to anticipate all the changes that could come about in a rapidly changing world.

This is of course a bit of an excuse, and, since the crisis, economists have been at work seeking to understand what happened, as well as looking for solutions that can enable economies to recover. It has also launched a debate on the way in which economics should be taught in universities, and this will be discussed in Chapter 10 of the book.

Some other challenges

There are many other topics on which economists can add to our understanding. Why do footballers earn so much – and command such enormous fees in the transfer market? How do we design policies to alleviate poverty in sub-Saharan Africa and other parts of the world? Why have firms become so concerned with their reputation and image – and how do we prevent tax evasion? Why should student tuition fees for higher education be charged at current levels? You may well meet these and many other questions during your economics programme.

Branches of economics

It is important to realise that universities do not only exist to teach undergraduates. They are also there to advance knowledge through research. Individual economics staff at universities specialise in a range of research areas, and where possible like to teach about their specialist areas. The remainder of this chapter describes some of the main areas of specialism. When you are choosing where you would like to study, some of these branches of economics may have particular interest to you, and you would be wise to explore the websites of your target universities to see whether they offer modules that cover your interests. You will find examples of all the following areas being offered somewhere in the country – but some are more common than others. They appear here in alphabetical order.

Behavioural economics

Do individuals always act rationally? Or are their decisions subject to influence by psychological, social or emotive factors? The growing sub-discipline of behavioural economics explores these issues, and analyses the implications for the operation of markets and resource allocation. The behaviour of firms and individual economic agents comes under scrutiny here. In some cases, modules in behavioural economics may offer opportunities to engage in economic experiments to cast light on the motivations of economic agents under laboratory conditions.

Business or managerial economics

Business economics focuses on the way in which firms operate, and on how the internal organisation of firms affects behaviour. It draws on economic theory to explore the different ways in which firms are organised, and how they take decisions about production techniques, pricing and output. There will also be discussion of how firms behave in the markets in which they operate. Managerial economics covers similar ground, with a greater emphasis on the behaviour of managers.

Development economics

This is a branch of economics that applies economic analysis to understanding the particular problems faced by less-developed countries (LDCs). Many LDCs confront the problem of trying to alleviate poverty in their population while facing severe shortage of resources and poorly developed markets. In many cases, they continue to rely heavily on primary production, and are experiencing rapid population growth. Enabling economic and human development that will allow LDCs to participate in the global economy, and tackling the problems of extreme poverty and inadequate provision of health care and education is one of the major global challenges.

Econometrics

If you enjoy statistics and are keen to test whether the real world behaves in the way that economic theory says that it should, then you might wish to follow modules in econometrics. Indeed, on many undergraduate programmes, you will find that this is a core part of your curriculum.

Economic history

This area of study looks back at the way the economy has developed through time. As has been set out in earlier chapters, the development of economic theory has gone hand-in-hand with the evolution of the economy. The path of the economy has been influenced by developments in economic analysis and policy, and economic thinking has had to develop to explain new changes occurring in the real world. An understanding of economic history contributes to our understanding of economic analysis, especially at the macroeconomic level.

Environmental economics

This branch of economics looks at how economic analysis can be applied to an understanding of the environment in which we live. It is not just about pollution and externalities, but also about the way in which we use renewable and non-renewable resources. It is of vital importance in today's world, and is an area in which economics interacts with other disciplines.

Financial economics

This differs from business economics in its focus on financial assets and monetary activities. In particular it looks at asset pricing, and the operation of financial markets such as the stock market and futures markets. It also explores the way in which stock market or banking 'bubbles' can develop, and at the importance of appropriate regulation of financial institutions, which has been brought into focus by the recent crisis. If you are set on a career in money and banking, or are interested in finance, this could be a module for you.

Health economics

As its name suggests, health economics looks at how economic analysis is applied to the health care sector. Some of the issues examined in this subject area were mentioned earlier in the chapter. The provision of health care is a key sector in the economy, but would not be efficiently provided in an unregulated market. Efficiency in the use of resources, and valuing health care resources are among the topics of interest here.

Heterodox economics

The main focus of the discussion of economic thinking in this volume has been what might be called 'mainstream' economics, in particular the neoclassical approach and the way in which that has evolved in more recent years. There has been a growing interest in alternative approaches, for example based on Marxian, post-Keynesian and feminist approaches among others. You may come across these alternative pluralist approaches under the name of heterodox economics. Alongside the more mainstream approaches, these alternative views offer interesting new perspectives on economic issues.

History of economic thought

Modules in the history of economic thought do what it says on the tin: they explore the evolution of economic thinking through studying the works of previous economists. Chapters 2, 4 and 5 introduced some of the core ideas of a selection of writers, but only scratched the surface. There is a growing belief in the economics profession that there is great value in studying the history of economic thought, so you are likely to find opportunities to pursue this topic.

Industrial economics

Like business economics, industrial economics focuses on the economic theory of the firm, exploring the operation of firms of all sizes, from the local corner shop to the massive multinational. It draws on game theory and other approaches to understand the strategic interaction of firms in a market. Industrial economics tends to be more 'technical' in its approach than business or managerial economics.

International economics

The importance of international trade in a globalised world economy offers a range of interesting topics, looking at the rationale for international trade, and the conditions under which countries can gain from specialisation and trade. It also looks at the patterns of world trade and how these have been affected by deregulation of goods and financial markets. The role of the World Trade Organisation and the impact of China's expansion are likely to figure in the discussions.

Labour economics

The study of labour markets incorporates a wide range of topics. The demand for labour by firms and the decisions on labour supply made by individual workers are the starting point for analysis, and show some significant differences from the operation of goods markets. Analysis sheds light on such topics as the causes and costs of unemployment, the impact of a minimum wage and the way in which wages are determined in a free market. This may help to explain why footballers receive such high earnings, whereas nurses and firefighters do not. The pattern of wages across occupations goes some way towards explaining the distribution of income in society and the pattern of inequality.

Mathematical economics

Economics uses mathematical techniques as a key tool of analysis, building models to represent reality. If you love mathematics, and want to see applications rather than pure mathematical theory, then a module in mathematical economics may suit you.

Political economy

Before the discipline became known as 'economics', it was referred to as 'political economy'. Political economy today stands at the junction between economics, politics, sociology, law and some other social sciences. It explores the relationship between these disciplines in casting light on the way in which economic outcomes are influenced by political, social and institutional factors. It may also investigate the way in which the choice and design of economic policy affect political and social institutions.

Public economics

An important area in economic analysis is the way in which the public sector works. Government fulfils many functions that are economic in nature, such as taxation, regulation, the provision of social services and administration of the law (for example in relation to property rights). The government may also intervene to stabilise the macroeconomy or to bail out financial institutions that are perceived to be too large to fail. The provision of infrastructure, law and order, defence or pensions support may also come under the government's remit. Public economics looks at the theory and practice of how and why governments intervene in the economy at both microeconomic and macroeconomic levels.

Regional/urban economics

In many economies such as the UK, there are significant differences between regions of the country in terms of economic performance. Average income may vary, and some regions consistently experience higher unemployment than others. In some countries (especially some less-developed countries), the differences between urban and regional areas are significant, and migration from rural to urban areas creates major tensions and problems. Modules in regional and urban economics examine the economic issues that underpin these differences.

Transport economics

As its name suggests, transport economics applies economic analysis to issues in the realm of transport. For example, road congestion is one problem that may require intervention in some form, as this can be viewed as an example of market failure in the form of an externality. Road pricing (charging drivers for using a congested road) is one way of tackling congestion, facilitated by advances in technology. However, there are broader issues that also need central coordination. Ideally, a country needs an integrated approach to transport policy, covering alternative modes of travel – road, rail and air. Each have differing environmental implications, so some central direction is needed to ensure that investment in new transport infrastructure is planned in the best interests of society.

Sub-disciplines in your degree

Most undergraduate programmes in economics are composed of a sequence of modules (or courses), which are likely to be a combination of compulsory core modules in microeconomics and macroeconomics, but with a choice of options. Depending on your particular chosen programme, most of the sub-disciplines outlined above are likely to be among the choice of options that you face. However, do not expect all of those listed to be available in every programme that is on offer. This could be an important issue for you when you are choosing your university and programme of study, especially if there are certain areas of economics that will fire your interest. The breadth of possibilities means there will be something for everyone, but it makes good sense to check that you can pursue your interests, whether that be environmental issues, finance or economic development. Chapter 10 will return to this issue.

References

Stern, N. (2006) *The Economics of Climate Change*. Cambridge: Cambridge University Press. Also available through the National Archives. A brief executive summary can be found at http://webarchive.nationalarchives.gov.uk/20130129110402/http://www.hm-treasury.gov.uk/media/9/9/CLOSED_SHORT_executive_summary.pdf

World Commission on Environment and Development (WCED) (1987) *Our Common Future*. Oxford: Oxford University Press.

PART III

Studying economics

8

The economist's toolkit

This chapter will:

- describe what it means to think like an economist
- highlight some key economic concepts that you will meet during your studies
- illustrate the use of diagrams in economic analysis
- discuss the role and importance of mathematics and statistical analysis in economics
- identify characteristics that would make you a good student of economics

Before joining an undergraduate programme in economics, it is a good idea to find out something about the tools that you will need to use in pursuing the subject. It is also important to know what attributes would stand you in good stead as you embark on your studies.

This chapter explores these issues, highlighting the way of thinking that you will develop as you study economics, and the use that will be made of diagrams, mathematics and statistics during the programme.

It is important to be aware that not all programmes are the same. This is partly in terms of the subject content that you study (although there is a common core of material specified by the QAA). However, it is also the case that programmes vary in the balance between theory, applied and technical content, and in the extent to which you can choose options as part of your degree. This means that it is advisable to take care when researching the various programmes on offer before choosing where to apply. The process of decision-making that you will need to go through in making good choices will be explored in Chapter 9.

Thinking like an economist

Economists often claim that the distinctive aspect of the subject is that is engenders a particular way of thinking about the world that sets it apart from other disciplines. This partly reflects the particular blend of using scientific method with the study of human behaviour. Furthermore, because so much of economic analysis is about decision-making, this can carry over into the everyday decisions that everyone has to make.

This 'way of thinking' is a tool that you will develop as you study the subject, but it is quite difficult to summarise before you have started. You will pick it up as you go, and suddenly find that it takes you over. However, one route into understanding what is involved is through exploring some of the fundamental concepts that underpin economic analysis.

Some of these concepts have already been introduced in earlier chapters. They are sometimes expressed as a sequence of **threshold concepts** that are seen as being central to the economics approach to problems and decisions. The following discussion of these is rather loosely based on the 15 threshold concepts set out in Sloman, Garratt and Wride (2014).

Choice and opportunity cost

As explained in Chapter 1, economic decisions are forced on us by scarcity. Resources are scarce, and choice between alternatives is at the heart of many economic decisions. Such a choice entails choosing the best among alternative possibilities, and the opportunity cost of the choice is the value of the next best alternative that is not chosen. Also important in this context is that sunk costs should not be taken into account when choosing. For example, if you have already paid for a ticket for a concert and cannot recoup the cost, this should not feature in deciding whether to attend it if a preferred option becomes available.

Markets

Markets can bring demand and supply into equilibrium, but may fail to meet social objectives.

Equilibrium is an important concept in economic analysis, and the demand and supply model shows that an equilibrium can be reached such that the quantity that consumers wish to buy is matched by the amount that suppliers wish to sell. This equilibrium comes about because both buyers and sellers respond to price signals.

This does not guarantee that the outcome is the best for society as a whole, as there are a number of reasons why there might be a form of market failure. Governments may sometimes be able to correct for this market failure and thus may be able to improve the way that resources are allocated – but intervention can sometimes fail to succeed in this objective.

Another important concept in relation to markets is the capacity to examine the impact of changes in market equilibrium through measuring **elasticity**. Elasticity measures the sensitivity of one variable to another: for example, the price elasticity of demand measures the sensitivity of quantity demanded of a good in response to a change in its price. This enables economic agents to anticipate the effect of a change in the economic environment.

The margin

Decisions may be taken by economic agents by considering marginal changes from the current position, which allows maximising behaviour.

Much neoclassical analysis rested on the assumption that economic agents act rationally. Consumers act to maximise utility, whereas firms act to maximise profits. This assumption says that economic agents act rationally. Recent developments in behavioural economics suggest that this may not always be the case.

Incentives and expectations

A further insight offered by economic analysis is that people respond to incentives, and may also be influenced by expectations.

This opens the possibility for economic agents (including government) to influence economic behaviour by taking actions that affect the incentives that motivate people, or to colour their expectations about the future.

Efficiency in resource allocation

Identifying what is an efficient overall allocation of resources has two dimensions. First, the output being produced should be produced as efficiently as possible in terms of the use of the inputs into production (productive efficiency). Second, the pattern of production should match the combination of goods and services that people wish to consume (allocative efficiency). With markets working perfectly across the whole society, a general equilibrium could be reached, at which point society would be as well-off as possible.

In reality, such a situation is not likely to occur. However, the possibility that an optimum could exist provides a benchmark against which we can evaluate how well markets are performing in reality.

Economic growth

At the macroeconomic level, there tend to be fluctuations in economic growth in the short run, in the form of business cycles. In the long run, economic growth occurs through an increase in the quantity of factors of production, or through an improvement in their productivity. In monitoring economic growth, it is crucial to distinguish between *real* and *nominal* changes.

Cumulative causation

Actions taken by economic agents can have knock-on effects that prolong their impact. A prime example of this is the Keynesian multiplier, by which an increase in spending can have multiplied effects.

More on thinking like an economist

It is not claimed that these concepts are exhaustive – for example, no mention was made of the way that people can gain through specialisation and trade. Nonetheless, they provide some guide to the way in which economists think. In particular, this applies to the approach that is taken to decision-making under the economics approach to problem-solving. There is a focus on identifying the way in which decisions are taken under assumptions about motivations and incentives. Being aware of opportunity cost may sharpen the way you think about decisions.

Diagrams

Chapter 3 used diagrams to introduce the demand and supply model. Diagrams are an important tool in economic analysis, and you will need to develop some facility in using (and producing) diagrams to illustrate economic ideas. Let us look at a few examples.

A production possibility frontier

Consider a farm that has a field that can be used to grow crops. On this field, the farm can either produce potatoes or Brussels sprouts – or a combination of the two. Given the size of the field, there is a limit to how many potatoes or Brussels sprouts can be grown. The situation is shown in Figure 8.1 in the form of a production possibility frontier (PPF), which is probably one of the first diagrams that you will meet when studying economics.

If the farm devotes all the field to producing Brussels sprouts, then point V on the figure shows the quantity of Brussels sprouts that can be produced. On the other hand, if only potatoes are produced, then production would be at point W. If the farm initially produces at V, but decides to produce some potatoes as well as tomatoes, some Brussels sprout production must be sacrificed (so the lost production of Brussels sprouts is the opportunity cost of producing more potatoes).

The curve labelled *PPF* shows the various combinations of the two crops that could be produced by making full use of the available resources. One

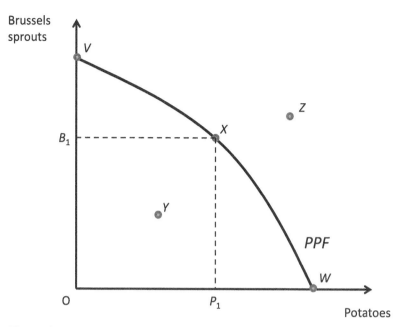

Figure 8.1 **A production possibility frontier.**

example is shown on the figure as point X, where the farm produces B_1 Brussels sprouts and P_1 potatoes.

The other points on the figure can also be interpreted. The point Y represents a position in which the farm is not using all of the available resources, as it could move to the right on the diagram and produce more potatoes without producing fewer Brussels sprouts, or could produce more Brussels sprouts while producing the original amount of potatoes by moving upwards. In other words, a point that is *inside* the *PPF* (such as Y) is regarded as inefficient, whereas a point along the frontier is efficient, because all resources are being utilised. On the other hand, point Z is unattainable, as it lies outside the frontier. Indeed, that is why it is called a frontier, as it shows the maximum combinations of the two goods that can be produced with existing resources.

This simple example shows how you need to become accustomed to interpreting points at different locations on a diagram.

Who bears the burden of an indirect tax?

The next example is a bit more complicated, and demonstrates how diagrams can be used for analysis as well as description. The task for which the diagram will be used is to analyse the effect on a market if the authorities impose a tax on sales of a good – in this case on cigarettes. We will compare the market

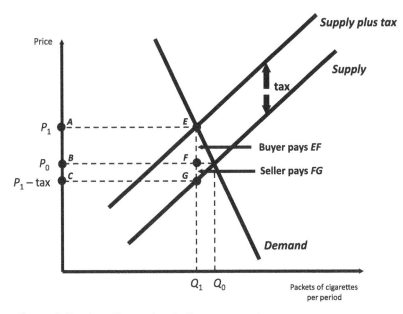

Figure 8.2 The effects of an indirect tax on cigarettes.

equilibrium with and without the tax, which is assumed to be of a fixed amount per packet. Figure 8.2 illustrates the situation.

Without the tax, the market equilibrium is found at the intersection of the *Demand* and *Supply* curves. This is with quantity at Q_0 and price P_0. This is the same as was set out in Chapter 3 when the demand and supply model was introduced.

Remember that the supply curve shows the quantity that firms are prepared to supply to the market at any given price. If the authorities impose a tax, the amount that firms receive from selling the good is less per packet because the tax must be paid, so the supply curve shifts by the amount of the tax. This is shown by the line '*Supply plus tax*' in the figure.

The new equilibrium in the market is now at point **E** on the diagram, where the *Demand* curve intersects *Supply plus tax*. The price has increased to P_1 and the quantity traded has fallen to Q_1. The revenue that the authorities receive from the tax is shown by the area **AEGC**. This is because the tax per packet is **AC** (or **EG**), so the total tax revenue is this quantity multiplied by the quantity, which is **AE** (or **CG**).

Notice that the price of cigarettes has not risen by the full amount of the tax. This suggests that when we compare the situation with and without the tax, the burden of paying the tax is shared between the buyers and the sellers. Buyers now pay P_1 instead of P_0, so their share of the tax per packet is **EF**.

Firms receive less per packet, so their share is **FG**. The way in which the tax burden is shared between buyers and sellers is determined by the shape of the demand curve. In this example, buyers are not very sensitive to price, so that they do not adjust their buying pattern very much. In other words, demand is highly inelastic. For this reason, they pay the higher share of the tax. This reflects the fact that smoking is addictive, and helps to explain why just imposing a tax on cigarettes is not enough to discourage smoking. This example shows how diagrams can help to analyse economic questions.

Mathematics and numeracy

Diagrams can help in the analysis of some economic questions, but suffer the limitation of being confined to two dimensions. Many economic issues are more complex than this, with several variables affecting things simultaneously. In such cases, mathematics offers an alternative approach.

Consider the demand and supply model, and the question of how the equilibrium price can be discovered. Earlier diagrams have shown both demand and supply curves as straight lines. In mathematical terms (as should be familiar from GCSE Maths), the form of equation for a straight line is:

$$Y = a + bX$$

where Y is the value on the y-axis, X is the value on the x-axis, a is the value of Y when X is zero (the point at which the line intersects the y-axis), and b is the slope of the line.

Suppose we know that the equation for the demand curve is given by:

$$Q_d = 16 - 5P$$

and supply is given by:

$$Q_s = 2 + 2P.$$

We can then find the value for the equilibrium price by setting these two equations equal to each other:

$$16 - 5P = 2 + 2P$$

It is then possible to solve this to find the value of P:

$$16 - 2 = 2P + 5P$$

i.e. $14 = 7P$, so $P = 2$.

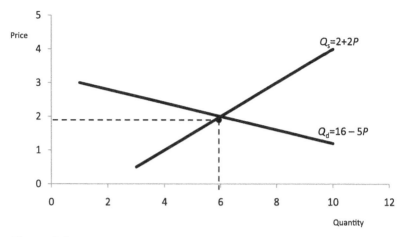

Figure 8.3 **Market equilibrium.**

This is the unique price at which demand equals supply given these demand and supply curves – in other words, this is the equilibrium price. You can confirm that this is the equilibrium by plotting the two equations on a graph: this is done in Figure 8.3.

You might think that this numerical example does not advance economic theory very far – and you would be right. However, the power of mathematics is not only in this sort of exercise. If we return to the general algebraic expression for a straight line, this could be generalised to a much more complex equation that brings in the other factors that influence the demand for a good, or could be varied to reflect the fact that the demand curve is not necessarily linear. By using algebraic manipulation it becomes possible to explore more complex aspects of the model and push the assumptions made to their logical conclusion. Those assumptions can then be evaluated against the original theory to establish their validity.

In addition to learning to use and apply mathematics, it will be important for you to be reasonably numerate – in other words, you may need to think about and to interpret numbers. A second example illustrates this.

Suppose there are two rival firms supplying a market, each setting price based on their expectations of what price the rival firm will set. Each firm can set either a high price or a low price, and each wants to maximise profits. However, the profit that each firm makes depends upon the actions of the rival firm. The matrix below summarises the possible outcomes, showing the profit made by each firm given the possible combinations of price choices. The profits made by Firm A are shown in circles.

		Firm A			
		High price		Low price	
Firm B	High price	(10)	10	(15)	2
	Low price	(2)	15	(5)	5

Suppose you are setting price on behalf of Firm A. The profit that you will make depends upon the price that Firm B will set. If Firm B sets a high price, you make either 10 units of profit if you also set price high or 15 if you choose a low price. If Firm B sets a price that is low, you make only 2 units of profit if you choose to set price high, or 5 units if you choose a low price. In either case, your preferred option is to set price low, as this brings higher profit whatever price is set by Firm B.

This is an example of game theory (a game known as the *Prisoner's Dilemma*, after the way in which this sort of game was first set out).

There are some further insights to be drawn from this game. Notice that Firm B faces exactly the same decision process, and will also choose to set a low price. Both firms thus make 5 units of profit. If they had been able to collude so that they both set a high price, they would each make twice as much profit. However, there would be an incentive for each to cheat. If Firm A knows that Firm B will set price to be low, it could make even more profits by setting a high price. This could lead Firm B to retaliate in the next period (assuming that Firm B did not also choose to cheat).

Statistics

The use of statistics is also important as a tool of economists, and requires different skills from those used in mathematics.

Data are important in economics, because they are the way in which the real world can be observed quantitatively. Some examples have already been seen earlier in the book, where graphs have been used to show the time-path of economic variables such as inflation and unemployment, or the relative levels of average income across countries in a particular year.

Figure 3.5 showed inflation in the UK in each year since 1860, which highlighted the key periods in which inflation rose and fell. Figure 5.1 showed GNI per capita in 2012 for selected countries. Graphs provide a simple but important way of monitoring the economic performance of a country, or undertaking international comparisons. They provide information that focuses attention on particular periods or countries.

It is often helpful to use graphs of data to look for patterns. For instance, it might be important to explore how different countries experienced the global recession that followed the financial crisis of the late 2000s. A time-series graph that brings together data on a number of countries is one approach, although showing more than a small number of countries can become confusing.

Figure 8.4 shows the annual growth rates of GDP for the UK, Greece, China and the world as a whole for the period 2000–2013.

You can see from this that the UK and Greece followed a similar pattern to the world as a whole until the onset of recession, although Greece showed a bit more variability in its growth rate. After 2009, the UK and the world showed a recovery, whilst Greece continued to suffer, with growth rates still negative right up to 2013. Meanwhile, China showed steady and rapid growth until 2007, and continued to see GDP growing even during and after the world recession. These sorts of patterns help us to understand what is going on in the world.

Another way of using data is to look for relationships between macro-economic variables. Keynes argued that there would be a positive relationship between consumers' expenditure and household income. A scatter graph can enable us to explore this relationship, as shown in Figure 8.5.

Each point marked on the graph shows the combination of consumption expenditure and income in a particular year. The pattern suggests that there is a strong positive relationship between these two variables, as overall there is an upward sloping pattern to the scatter, which is not too far away from a straight line. The relationship is not perfect, but it would be expected that it would be, as there are no doubt other factors than income that influence consumption expenditure. Nonetheless, the closeness of the pattern suggests that there is a close association between these variables.

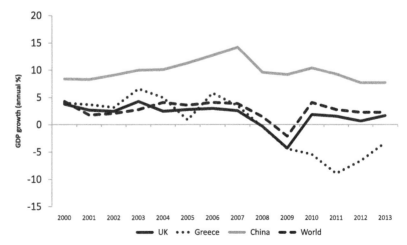

Figure 8.4 Annual growth rates, selected countries, 2000–13 (*Source:* Data from World Bank *World Development Indicators*).

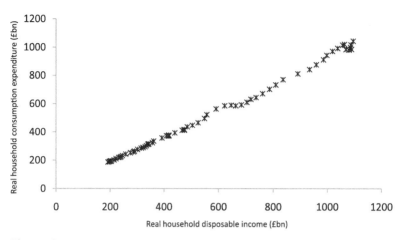

Figure 8.5 **Real consumption and income, 1948–2014 (*Source:* Based on data from the Office for National Statistics licensed under the Open Government Licence v.3.0. Data from ONS database).**

It is important to be aware that statistics can be misused by people pursuing a particular line of argument or viewpoint. Your degree will raise your awareness of how this is done, and how to spot when commentators are presenting data in a biased way to support their own arguments. For example, manipulating the scale of a graph can exaggerate or minimise the variation in a series, and thus alter your perceptions of how it is changing through time.

Econometrics takes this analysis further, using statistical techniques to estimate the line that would best fit the scatter of points, and to test its significance. It also allows the estimation of more complex relationships involving multiple variables, and adjusting for various complications that can arise in the process.

At university, you will have good access to data, either through Bloomberg terminals or databases such as the Office for National Statistics or the World Bank's *World Development Indicators*. You will also find that there is some excellent software that handles the computational aspects of statistical analysis, but you will need to provide the vision that allows economic ideas to be turned into testable hypotheses and the ability to interpret the results that you obtain. Your familiarity with this software will be an advantage in the job market.

What characteristics make a good student of economics?

Given this set of tools that economists bring to bear on economic issues, what characteristics do you need as you embark on an undergraduate degree in economics? In considering this, remember that it is your potential to develop the economist's approach that matters at this stage. Your chosen programme will provide the opportunities for you to develop the skills as you proceed. Chapter 10 will explore more carefully how your programme of study is likely to be organised, and what it will contain. However, there are some key pointers that may help you to decide whether economics will suit you.

Enthusiasm

Whatever subject you choose to study at university, it is really important that you begin with enthusiasm for it. If you are going to spend three (or four) years in intensive study, an enthusiasm for the subject is crucial for you to maintain momentum.

This may be difficult in the case of economics if you have not studied it before you set out. However, it helps if you have an active interest in wanting to understand how society works, especially in its economic aspects.

Adopting a scientific approach

To study economics successfully, you need to be prepared to adopt a social science perspective, relying on evidence and analysis above assertion and instinct. It also helps if you are ready to be objective, standing back from personal beliefs and interests to recognise the rigour of economic analysis and apply it to real-world situations.

It helps to be able to adopt a logical approach to problems, although there are also times when a dash of creativity may lead you to novel solutions. You will need to learn to use language in a precise way – and to take on board the economists' use of jargon.

It is also important that you learn to be critical and evaluative in your analysis, recognising logical flaws in arguments, or being aware of situations in which data are being manipulated.

Skills development

As this chapter has pointed out, economists use certain tools to investigate problems and theories. You need to be prepared to learn to use and interpret graphs and diagrams, and to be ready to develop the mathematical skills required for economic analysis. Your programme will also help you to develop critical thinking and the ability to be evaluative in your judgements. Remember that not all degree programmes in economics are the same, and that the balance of mathematic content varies between institutions.

The next chapter explores some of the ways in which you can select a degree programme that will suit you, and how you can prepare for the transition into higher education.

Reference

Sloman, J., Garratt, D. and Wride, A. (2014) *Economics*, 9th edn. Harlow: Pearson Education.

9

Preparing for university

This chapter will:

- discuss the choices facing you when preparing to apply to university
- provide guidance on how to decide between alternative economics programmes
- highlight key sources of information that help you to focus on programmes that match your preferences
- discuss how you can prepare for studying economics at university – which is very different from what you will be experiencing at school or college

To make the best use of your time at university, you need to be well prepared. There are important choices to be made before you put in your application, and there are steps you can take to see that you arrive ready to take full advantage of your opportunity. Your time at university will offer you consumption benefits – new friends and new opportunities for leisure activities – but it is also a form of investment in your future human capital. It makes sense to do everything you can to make sure that your investment brings a sound rate of return. This chapter explores some of the ways in which you can be ready to maximise your return.

Choices

When you begin to consider applying to university, you face a classic economic decision. You are confronted with scarcity, as the UCAS form allows you to select and apply for a limited number of programmes. Opportunity cost enters the picture. If you choose one particular set of options, you forgo the possibility of applying for others. If you choose to apply for single honours programmes in economics, you exclude other possibilities such as nursing or dentistry.

It may help to think of this initial stage as involving three key choices:

- You need to choose which subject (or combination of subjects) to study.
- You need to select the universities to which you will apply.
- You need to choose the particular programmes at your chosen universities, as most offer several pathways and combinations.

The choices that you make are all important decisions that can change your life. So how do you get it right? The choice is yours, and you need to tailor your decisions to your own attributes and preferences.

For some, the choice of subject is easily made. Some people decide at a very early age what they want to be when they grow up, whether to be a doctor, musician or engineer. However, professional economist tends not to figure strongly in the list of those early choices!

There are others who start by choosing the location (place or university) where they want to study, and then look to see what subjects and programmes are on offer. For example, some students like to be able to live at home while they are studying, or close to where they work so they can study part-time. Perhaps the choice of university is dictated by where a boy- or girlfriend is studying. The notion of opportunity cost may be especially significant here, as decisions limit the range of options available. You could end up studying a subject that does not interest you for the sake of a relationship that turns out to be short lived.

In reality, of course, these three choices are interconnected. They need to be made simultaneously to reach the best combined solution. However, the variety of available choices is vast, given the number of possible subjects, universities and programmes. A structured approach is needed to make sense of it all.

Choosing a subject

In good economist fashion, let's begin by making an assumption – that choosing your subject is the first step. If for whatever reason you have chosen your university already, then you still need to choose a subject, but may be choosing from a more limited range of options.

If you are reading this book, and have got this far with it, it is a fair guess that you are seriously considering studying economics.

What is your motivation? You may be considering university-level economics because you think it will be interesting, or that it is an important subject for society – and I would not argue with those sentiments. You may have heard about the financial crisis or other economic events that have hit the headlines, and want to understand how the economy works. Perhaps you have enjoyed studying the subject at A-level or other pre-university course and want to continue with it. Or perhaps you believe that you have the attributes that are needed so that you will be successful and get a good degree.

The *Economics Network* is located at the University of Bristol, and was previously the Subject Centre for Economics for the Higher Education Academy. The Network has interviewed a range of university economics students to find out why they chose to study economics, and you can find a selection of these interviews on their website at http://whystudyeconomics.ac.uk/. Among these students, one of the most popular reasons given for studying economics was to make money. (Chapter 12 will comment on the employment options open to economics graduates.)

Whatever your motivation, you need to find a degree programme that will meet your expectations and deliver what you want.

The popularity of economics

At this point, you might be interested in how many students have chosen to study economics in the UK. Data are available on this from the Higher Education Statistics Agency (HESA). Figure 9.1 shows the number of students studying economics in UK universities in each year since 2002/03. This

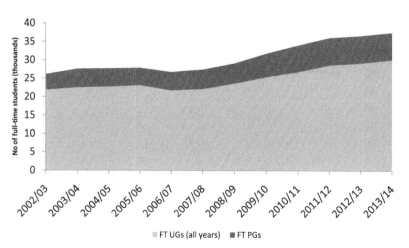

Figure 9.1 Number of students studying economics in UK universities (*Source:* Data from HESA Student Record 2002/03–2013/14 https://www.hesa.ac.uk/free-statistics).

101

focuses on full-time students, and distinguishes between undergraduate and postgraduates.

You can see that the numbers of students studying economics held fairly steady until about 2007/08, after which the number of undergraduates increased steadily. Overall student numbers were also expanding in this period, so it is interesting to see how the numbers studying economics followed the national trend.

Figure 9.2 explores this by using index numbers, based on the year 2002/03 as the base. It shows the number of full-time undergraduates in each year relative to the number in the base year, comparing economics with the total for all subjects. The number studying economics has increased relative to the total in the latter part of the period. Compared with 2002/03, there were 5% more undergraduates overall in 2013/14; for economics, however, there were 38% more. In other words, economics has seen a surge in popularity relative to other subjects.

An article in the Royal Economic Society's newsletter (Johnston and Reeves, 2015) noted that this increase was not even across the higher education sector, with a notable difference between the 'new' universities (those that achieved university status after 1992) and the older institutions. In other words, the increase in the number of economics students was mainly the result of expansion in the 'old' (pre-1992) universities, whereas the 'new' (post 1992) universities remaining more or less constant, with some withdrawing some of their economics degrees.

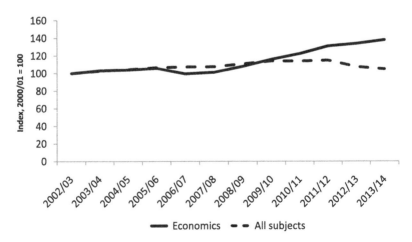

Figure 9.2 Index of full-time undergraduate student numbers (2002/03=100) (*Source:* Author's calculations, based on data from HESA Student Record 2002/03–2013/14).

Finding a focus

Having decided that you want to study economics, how do you find the best available programme to suit you? After all, there are hundreds of alternative possibilities out there. Picking your way through the labyrinth of information on the internet requires a structured approach.

If your sights are firmly fixed on a future as an economist in the academic world, the Government Economic Service or in economics research, then you will probably look for a single honours programme, which will prepare you for postgraduate work in economics. A degree that focuses closely on economics will also prepare you for a variety of alternative occupations, which will be discussed in Chapter 12.

If you prefer to combine your study of economics with the study of another subject, then you may wish to find a joint honours programme, in which you divide your time between two different disciplines. If this is your chosen option, then the next step is to choose your second subject. The variety of combinations on offer is wide, as was discussed in Chapter 6.

One approach to choosing a second subject is to pick one that matches your particular interests or intended career. Or there may be a subject that you especially enjoyed studying at school or college. Following a subject in which you have a keen interest is beneficial, because you are more likely to perform well, as compared to something that you find tedious or boring. Furthermore, learning to approach a question or problem in different ways can make you a more flexible thinker, which can be an advantage in today's rapidly changing world.

In choosing to follow your interests in this way, consider how well the two subjects will fit together. If your enthusiasm is mathematics, then the connections with economics would make this a powerful combination. On the other hand, if your preferred second subject is more remote from economics, you may find yourself being pulled in different directions by having to study in different ways in the two halves of your degree.

You may choose your second subject on other grounds. There may be particular skills that you would like to develop, or there may be a certain career that you believe could be enhanced by studying a combination of subjects. For example, if you are hoping for a career in politics, then studying a combination of economics with politics or international relations would be a sensible choice. If you are intent on a career in finance or management, then combining your study of economics with finance or management (respectively) would be a coherent decision.

With these decisions made, you have at least begun to restrict the available options a bit. If you are sure that you just want to study economics by itself, or that you want to find a joint degree with a particular second subject, you will have made your choice a bit more manageable – but will still find a wide range of potential programmes. It is time to explore the information that is out there.

Research and information gathering

An important website to help you to find your preferred degree programme is the Unistats site at https://unistats.direct.gov.uk/find-out-more/key-information-set. This brings together information in the form of a Key Information Set (KIS) about every undergraduate degree programme offered in the UK. However, if you type 'economics' into its search engine, you will be offered a list of more than a thousand possible courses (programmes). This is why it makes sense to focus your searching as the first step.

In passing, be careful how you use the search engine. For example, if you are looking for a joint honours degree in Economics and Politics, avoid just typing 'Economics Politics', which produces a list of degrees that contain *either* economics or politics in the title, which covers more than 2,000 possibilities. Entering 'Economics and Politics' produces just over 100, which is more manageable.

How else can you build a shortlist?

Choosing a university

There are more than a hundred universities in the UK offering a degree that includes economics. What criteria should you use in compiling your shortlist?

One possible filter is location. How close to home do you want to be? This comes down to your personal preferences. Some students like to be close to home, and thus choose a university within a relatively small radius of their home town. Others may be ready to taste the freedom of being away from home. Others may want to be far enough to feel that freedom, but yet be close enough to feel secure. If your home is in Penzance (in Cornwall), you might feel that the north of Scotland is a step too far.

The University of Wolverhampton has provided a useful interactive map showing the location of higher education institutions in the UK. You can find this at http://www.scit.wlv.ac.uk/ukinfo/index.php. This provides links to the universities' own websites and to other information about each institution.

An important point to remember is that universities are in competition with each other to attract students. Their websites are designed to highlight their strengths and their objectives – and also their distinctiveness.

One way in which universities may differ is in the balance of their activities. All universities carry out both teaching and research, but the balance between these aspects of their work varies between institutions, as does the extent of enterprise or engagement with businesses. University websites may provide some hints about this – look for their mission statements.

You may be aware that there are some so-called 'mission groups', in which universities have come together to promote their common interests. The

Russell Group brings together more than 20 universities that state that they are:

> committed to maintaining the very best research, an outstanding teaching and learning experience and unrivalled links with business and the public sector.
>
> http://www.russellgroup.ac.uk/

These universities tend to describe themselves as being research-intensive, with a strong focus on their strengths in this activity.

The University Alliance is a group of about 20 universities that prides itself on its 'links, connections and partnerships with industry and the professions'.

> We are universities with a common mission to make the difference to our cities and regions. We use our experience of providing high quality teaching and research with real world impact to shape higher education and research policy for the benefit of our students, and business and civic partners.
>
> http://www.unialliance.ac.uk/

The Million+ group sees itself as a university think tank aiming to influence government policy. Its affiliates are drawn from higher education institutions that gained the university designation after 1992.

> http://www.millionplus.ac.uk/

How does this help you to build your shortlist? Joining a research-intensive university brings you into contact with economists who are working at the frontiers of knowledge of the subject, which may mean that the institution builds a strong reputation with the public. On the other hand, the opportunities for industry experience may be more established at some other institutions, and some of the newer universities offer more flexible and innovative programmes, or may be better geared towards part-time study. There is a danger here of over-generalisation, as the nature of universities within the groups varies substantially. Nonetheless, the groups do bring together like-minded universities, which may help to narrow your choices.

League tables

University league tables such as *The Complete University Guide*, the *Guardian University Guide* and the *Sunday Times Good University Guide* offer rankings of universities for the main subject areas, including economics. Universities tend to express scepticism about these (even when they perform well), as it is so difficult to boil down the components of a good degree into a single number.

However, universities also take steps to maintain or improve their position, reflecting the competition to attract good students.

The league tables may be helpful in helping you to identify where you want to study (subject to all your other preferences, of course). However, to get the most out of them, you should look not only at the overall average score, but at the component elements that contribute to the total. Notice also that the tables use different components to reach their overall rankings, so it is important to consider what the individual scores say about the things that you hold to be significant.

Using the KIS

Once you have drawn up a shortlist of universities and programmes, it is time to visit the Unistats site to consult the Key Information Set (KIS), as mentioned earlier. If you visit the site and click on a particular programme, you will find a standardised set of information.

The first section brings in results from the *National Student Survey*, in which students are asked to comment on their level of satisfaction with their course. The scores on the individual components vary across the questions asked, so do not judge a single institution in isolation, but compare it with other universities that you are considering. In particular, notice that scores on feedback tend to be less strong than on other aspects, so do not judge the response to these questions too quickly.

The KIS goes on to provide information about employability, including average salary after six months, a summary of what students are doing six months after finishing their course (including those who have gone on to further study), and the sorts of jobs they are doing. The KIS also provides data about fees and living costs.

Information is provided about the time spent on lectures, seminars and independent study, as well as the balance of assessment between coursework and written examinations. Finally, there is data from the *National Student Survey* about how students rate their Students' Union.

The KIS website allows you to build a shortlist of courses, so that you can compare them side-by-side. In each section, the university can provide links to its own website to explain things in more detail.

Learning from university websites

Once you have your shortlist, you will want to visit the relevant university websites. These will give you a fuller picture of their degree programmes. There are some key things that are worth seeking out.

One important piece of information to find is the level of offer that will be made for you to enter the programme. Given that universities are competing with each other, the level of offer (the price of entry) may be an indicator of the level of demand. A high offer level may indicate a high level of demand for the programme. It may indicate that the university is intent on restricting entry to the best students – and that it can attract the students that it needs at that level. This may influence your decision in various ways. A high offer level may encourage you to apply because this may indicate a high quality programme – or it may deter you if you do not expect to reach those grades.

Be aware also that some economics degree programmes (an increasing number) require A-level mathematics (or equivalent) as an entry qualification. If you do not have this, you will need to look for programmes that do not insist on it. Chapter 10 will explain how you will acquire the mathematical skills that you need once you start your programme.

It is also worth searching out the staff list for the economics department. By looking at their profiles, you will get some feel for the sort of research interests that members of academic staff are pursuing. These pages are easier to find on some university websites than others.

Check out the programme structure (this will be discussed further in Chapter 10), and dip into the module profiles if these are accessible. If you are interested in particular sub-disciplines of economics, such as environmental, industrial or development economics, check whether the university you are considering offers optional modules in those areas, and look closely at those module profiles to see more detail about what will be covered. This will give you a good feel for whether this will capture your interest.

Visit or open days

Most universities offer visit or open days, when potential students can visit the campus to find out more about the university and its programmes. There may be general open days, when anyone can visit, or here may be visits designed for students who have applied or have accepted places. This is a really important part of your decision process, as you can learn a lot from visiting the campus and its surroundings.

The general environment of a university is important, because if you are going to live there for the three years of your studies, it needs to be an environment in which you can be comfortable. Otherwise you will not give of your best or perform as you can.

The best way you can find out about what it is like to study at a place is to talk to students who have already experienced it. Make the most of the opportunity to do this. They will tell you about the strengths and the weaknesses of the academic and the social life. They can talk from a unique perspective as, being current students experiencing the programme, they *know* what it is like.

Talk to the academic staff. Quiz them about things; see how well they interact with you. Be ready with questions that *you* want to ask, do not be content with what the staff think you want to know. "Useful questions to ask at an open (visit) day" (page 137) provides you with some questions that you might ask when on campus. Choose the ones that relate to your own curiosity, and ask both students and staff. (See if you get the same answers!)

In short, find out as much as you can so that you can make a truly informed choice. If you have narrowed your choice down to a very short list, but find little difference between the academic content of the programmes, then you should take into account the environment of the place, and think where you will be most comfortable.

Transitions and preparations

Once you have settled on a choice of universities and accepted an offer, what can you then do in order to be ready for university?

One important thing to remember as you make the transition from school or college to university is that higher education is simply different. There will be differences in the approach to learning and teaching. One of the most important aspects of a university education is that you will need to become an independent learner. Do not expect your lecturers to tell you everything that you need to know. They will provide you with a starting point, but you will then need to discover how you can learn for yourself.

This helps to explain why the time you spend in formal contact with lecturing staff in lectures or classes is much smaller as a proportion than you will have experienced earlier in your educational life. You will no doubt have noticed this when you looked at the KIS website. This also explains why the nature of feedback that you will receive on your work will be very different. Becoming aware of this is an important part of the transition to higher education – and this is true in most subjects, although the balance between formal and independent study hours may vary a bit.

When preparing for an economics degree programme, it is helpful to realise that no UK economics programme requires A-level economics as an entry qualification, so you will not be expected to know anything about the subject when you begin. Chapter 10 will discuss how university economics programmes deal with this.

Although no formal training in economics is required, there are ways you can prepare. Follow news about economic events in the media. Read the serious press discussions about economic affairs. You might read *The Economist*. If your college library has copies of the magazine *Economic Review*, dip into that (this is a magazine written for students meeting economics for the first time).

Students often contact universities to find out which textbooks will be used during their first year, thinking this might be a good way of preparing for study. The Additional resources section (page 147) provides a list of some of the most popular textbooks. However, this may not be the best way to start. Textbooks are not designed for this purpose, and they are probably not the best way to start. However, there are now several books that talk about economic issues in novel and informal ways, introducing the approach that economists take to problems without the theoretical details. These provide a readable introduction to economic discussions, and are well worth reading. You will find an annotated bibliography of these alongside the textbooks in the Resources section.

In all of these preparations, watch for the topics that you find especially interesting, whether it be poverty, the environment, the economy's performance, the behaviour of firms or migration. Make use of the internet to discover more.

Reference

Johnston, J. and Reeves, A. (2015) *The Rise of Elitism in Economics. Royal Economic Society Online Newsletter* 169(April). Available at http://www.res.org.uk/view/art2bApr15Features.html

10

Economics at university

- try to give you a flavour of what it will be like to study economics at university
- discuss the process of transition from school or college to higher education, and the information that will be provided to you at the start
- describe the structure of the academic year
- set out how the curriculum content is likely to be delivered
- discuss the curriculum content that you can expect and the way it is likely to be organised
- highlight changes to university teaching of economics in the wake of the financial crisis
- identify the modes of assessment and feedback that are typical in an economics programme
- explain the meaning and importance of independent study

You have chosen to study economics, either by itself or alongside another subject. You have prepared a shortlist of degree programmes, applied and got your place. You have prepared as best you can. What will it be like? This chapter discusses what you should expect from your programme of study.

In considering this issue, it is important to remember that there are many differences between institutions, and differences in the preferences of the students that attend them. This chapter can only offer general guidance, and is intended to help you to make your own decision, rather than direct you towards particular types of institution.

The beginnings

When you first arrive on campus, there is likely to be initial confusion. You will be meeting new people, looking for lecture and seminar rooms and having lots of information thrown at you (which you will probably forget). Don't panic: it will all become clear in time. There will be handbooks and plenty of information available online, and good access to computing facilities.

All universities have support services that will provide advice and guidance for you, and you are likely to be allocated a personal tutor who will be available to provide advice on academic matters (such as your choices of optional modules), and who can point you to other specialist support services in the university. Do take advantage of these support services, and get to know your personal tutor – remember that when you near the end of your studies, you will need to obtain academic references to support your job applications. If your tutor knows you, he or she can provide a more personal reference than if the only information available relates to your academic performance.

Along with your offer of a place, you will have received details of the contents of your programme and the fees. This may take the form of a document known as a *programme specification*, which is a formal document that sets out how your programme is organised and the outcomes that it is designed to deliver. This is provided on the advice of the Competition and Markets Authority, which is keen to ensure that students get all the information that they need about their proposed course of study. You will find that for many universities, these programme specifications are publicly available through their websites.

In many universities in the UK, the first year is known as a 'qualifying' year. This means that you need to pass it in order to progress to the next year, but the results and grades that you obtain will not count towards your final degree award. Don't be taken in by this. If you choose to coast your way through the first year because all you need to do is to pass, you will find yourself ill-prepared for the second year – which does count.

This is especially true in economics. If you have not studied economics before, then it is vital to gain a sound foundation in the subject before you move to the more difficult material that you will meet in year 2.

If you have studied economics before, perhaps at A-level, then there are enormous dangers in being complacent in the first year, only to find that you have not appreciated the differences in approach that become increasingly significant as you proceed. In particular, you need to be aware that the approach to learning and teaching in economics at university entails much more use of mathematics, and you need to get used to that.

Student societies

When you arrive at university, you will be deluged by student societies wanting to recruit you. These typically cater for a wide range of sporting and social activities, and are an excellent way of meeting like-minded fellow students. However, watch also for societies that are related to economics. There may be a society run for economics students, or you may find societies such as AISEC or Enactus that are geared towards encouraging professional leadership or enterprise. These are international student societies with global networks that you can tap into.

The timing of your degree

Most economics degree programmes in England and Wales follow the traditional three-year pattern leading to a Bachelor's degree. At some universities you can study economics in a sandwich format, taking one year away from the university in a work environment to gain experience. You may also be able to go for a year abroad as part of a joint degree with a modern language. This is something to look for if you find this an attractive proposition.

You may also be able to go abroad as an exchange student for a term or semester. This does not add to the overall length of your degree; you would normally study in an overseas institution, following similar modules to those that you would have studied if you had stayed at your 'home' university.

A few universities are now beginning to offer an accelerated programme, in which you can finish your degree in just two years. The KIS website also lists a very small number of degree programmes in England where you spend four years in undergraduate study, with the fourth year made up of master's level modules. You then graduate with an MEcon (Honours), having received four years of student loans, having studied economics in more depth, with some experience of study at the postgraduate level.

In Scotland, programmes are four years in duration, but you may be able to join the programme in the second year if you have the requisite entry qualifications. However, you end up with a Master's degree, rather than a Bachelor's.

The timing of your academic year can be organised in different ways, depending on which university you attend. Some use a three-term system, with breaks at Christmas and Easter. Some organise the formal teaching in two semesters per year, in some cases spread over three terms. You can check how the pattern works for your university by visiting their website. It is probably wise to find out when examinations take place. Again, this varies between universities; you may find there are mid-year exams, or you may face exams only at the end of each year.

In most cases, your learning will be delivered in a number of modules – although these may be known as 'courses' at some universities. The number of these varies between institutions, so you may find yourself following 4, 5, 6 or 8 modules per year, in some cases up to 11 or 12.

For most programmes, you accumulate credits as you complete your various modules. These may be expressed in the UK system of CATS (Credit

Accumulation and Transfer Scheme) or in the European system of ECTS (European Credit Transfer and Accumulation System). You do not need to worry about this too much, but it may be helpful to be aware that there is an expectation that the number of credits attached to a module will be associated with a number of hours of study, normally totalling about 40 hours per week, which gives you an indication of how much effort you are expected to put into your studies. Notice that this is not only for economics, but for all subjects.

The way in which these study hours are made up varies between disciplines and between universities. Your study hours will be divided between lectures, classes, seminars, workshop and tutorials, etc., and independent (guided) study. This is where you will see a major difference between school/college and higher education.

Lectures typically involve relatively large groups of students – in some cases numbering in the hundreds. Lectures bring together all of the students following a module, and are designed for your lecturers to provide information and guidance about module content. Lectures will typically provide the basics of the material needed on the module, but will leave you to reflect and fill in the details afterwards, using further reading and exercises to build your understanding.

Learning to take good notes on lectures is a key skill that you will need to develop as soon as possible. Having good notes for revision is invaluable, and active note-taking means that you will assimilate the material much better. It also helps you to concentrate during lectures.

Technology is beginning to change the way in which lectures are used. You are likely to find that some lecturers will provide online videos for you to watch before you attend the lecture, and will set aside part of the time for open questions and discussion. You may also find that lectures are recorded and made available to you online afterwards. This is not to save you having to attend (watching a 50-minute video on your computer is not a rewarding experience in itself). However, the recordings are valuable in allowing you to revisit parts of the lecture where you need to think more deeply about the content and to add to your notes.

Classes, seminars, workshops and tutorials (terminology varies between universities) provide opportunities for you to learn in smaller groups. They may take various forms. On mathematical, statistics or technical modules, you may have to work through exercises, with a tutor available to answer your questions in the class sessions. In other seminars you may engage in discussion on key topics, or find yourself participating in interactive role play. There may also be sessions that introduce approaches to problem-solving. You may find information on this in the module profiles on the university website.

The balance between the various styles of formal contact will vary between modules, and across the years of your programme, as will the balance between formal contact time and independent study. Learning how to be independent is a crucial part of all university learning and teaching, and you are likely to find that independent study becomes more important as your study progresses through the years. You can find information about this balance on the KIS website, as it is one of the key indicators provided for each programme.

It is also worth noting that there is evidence to suggest that attendance at lectures and other learning opportunities has a significant effect on student achievement, so don't fall into the habit of thinking that you can compress all your studying into the last few weeks before exams. The more you put into your studies, the better will be your results at the end.

Curriculum content

Your programme modules will typically include a set of core modules that ensures that you meet the requirements of the QAA subject benchmark (2015), which sets out the expected subject knowledge and understanding to be provided ('usually') by single honours degree programmes in economics, which are worth citing in full here:

i   Economic concepts, principles and tools, the understanding of which might be verbal, graphical and/or mathematical. These concepts, tools and principles play a key role in reasoning. They address the microeconomic issues of decision and choice, the production and exchange of goods, the pricing and use of inputs, the interdependency of markets, the relationships between principals and agents, and economic welfare. They also include the macroeconomic issues of employment, national income, the balance of payments, the distribution of income, economic growth, financial and business cycles, and the role of money creation, banking and the financial system in the economy, society and the environment.

ii Economic policy at both the microeconomic and macroeconomic levels. In all these, students show an understanding of analytical methods and model-based argument and understand different methodological approaches and their strengths and limitations.

iii Relevant quantitative methods and computing techniques. These include appropriate mathematical and statistical methods, including econometrics. Students have exposure to the use of such techniques on actual economic, financial or social data, using suitable statistical or econometric software.

iv The nature, sources and uses of both quantitative and qualitative data and an ability to select and apply appropriate methods that economists might use to analyse such data.

v   The applications of economics. Students discover how to apply relevant economic principles and reasoning to a variety of applied topics. They are also aware of how economics can be applied to design, guide and interpret commercial, economic, social and environmental policy. As part of this, they have the ability to discuss and analyse government policy and to evaluate the performance of the UK and other economies, past and present.

http://www.qaa.ac.uk/en/Publications/Documents/
SBS-Economics-15.pdf

The way in which these are delivered in an economics degree programme is normally by providing modules in microeconomics, macroeconomics, mathematics and statistics/econometrics. In most programmes, there will be modules in the first year that lay the foundations in each of these areas. You may find that students on the economics modules will be streamed in the early part of the programme based on whether they have studied A-level economics or not. Similarly, where A-level mathematics is not an entry requirement, there may be separate teaching of maths and statistics to ensure that students are at similar levels of knowledge and understanding by the end of the first year.

In addition to this core material, you will probably have to choose optional modules, which may be in sub-areas of economics, in other closely related disciplines, such as accounting, business or politics, or in interdisciplinary modules that allow you to learn about alternative approaches to problems. The extent to which there is flexibility in the curriculum varies significantly across universities, but there is an increasing trend to encourage interdisciplinary learning, which is seen to be valuable in the workplace. Remember that your personal tutor will be able to offer advice to guide you in your choices.

The CORE project

Following the financial crisis of the late 2000s, there was much public debate about the teaching of economics in universities, partly initiated by students at the University of Manchester, who formed the *Post-Crash Economics Society* in 2011. The impetus for this reflected the feeling that students were being well-trained in the technicalities of the subject, but were not necessarily well-prepared for understanding how the real world operates.

An international collaboration of 25 economists, led by Professor Wendy Carlin at University College London, set up the Curriculum Open-access Resources in Economics (CORE) project to produce new teaching resources that would create a broader economics curriculum. At the heart of this approach is the notion that the starting point for teaching economics should be evidence rather than theory, and that students should be provided with the tools needed to analyse and explain what they observe, approaching economic issues in a context that encompasses social, political, ethical and behavioural considerations.

What does this mean for you? It may mean that you will experience this approach to learning economics, as it is being piloted at a number of universities in the UK and other countries around the world. Even if your chosen university is not (yet) adopting the programme, the discussion has aroused a lot of debate in the academic economics profession, which is likely to inject more dynamism into your curriculum.

Assessment and feedback

The National Student Survey (NSS) results show that students across the country are concerned about assessment and (especially) feedback. This partly reflects the different approach to assessment and feedback as compared with school/college.

A first thing to realise about assessment is that each university designs its own forms of assessment, and sets its own examination questions. There is no central body that does this on their behalf. Furthermore, you will be marked by the staff who teach you. There are external examiners who will check the assessment process, but the marks are awarded by your own lecturers and their colleagues. This means that assessment tasks vary between institutions – indeed, they also vary between modules at the same institution.

On your economics programme, you will face a variety of different forms of assessment. Unseen written examinations will almost certainly form part of the assessment, but you will also be required to undertake coursework, which itself may take a variety of forms. On the mathematical modules, you will need to solve problems and exercises. In statistics you will undertake problems in estimation and the evaluation of evidence. In other modules, you will write essays, prepare project briefs or reviews of journal articles. You may have to produce presentations or even a film or website. On some modules, you may find yourself working in groups with other students. These are all designed to help you to obtain skills that you may need as an economist in the work environment.

On many programmes, you will have the opportunity to carry out some economics research, reporting this in the form of a project report or dissertation. This will normally take place in your final year of study, and will be supervised by a member of the academic staff. This can be a very rewarding part of your degree, as it is a chance to investigate a topic of interest to you, and to do so in some depth. It will often count as two modules in the final year, and is an opportunity for you to show what you have learned during your degree, and your ability to apply economic analysis. It is also provides a topic that you can discuss in job interviews, backed up with the report itself to show your qualities. Think of this as an opportunity to showcase what you have learnt during your degree programme.

If you look on the KIS website, you will find a link for 'Assessment methods explained', which will tell you about the way in which you will be assessed on your particular programme.

You will find that the feedback you receive will come in a variety of forms. At school/college you may have been accustomed to receive feedback in the form of written comments on your submitted essays. Although you may still receive this sort of feedback, in the higher education context, feedback comes in many other ways, for example in the form of direct interaction with your lecturers, or in the classes and seminars that you attend. This is all part of you becoming a more independent learner.

One aspect of your assessment that you will be especially interested in is the way in which your results are combined to produce your overall degree result.

The rules for progressing from one year of study to the next vary between institutions. You may find that you need to pass every module, or that you can compensate for failure in one module by performing well in others. Of course, you should not set out on your study with the intention of failing anything! However, you should make sure that you understand the rules.

You may even need to be aware of what will happen if you do fail, and need to retake some modules. Understanding this may provide an incentive for you to work hard in order to avoid this outcome! The best way of avoiding the need to retake is to work consistently through the year and make sure that you understand tricky topics as you go. If you leave everything to the last minute you may find yourself in danger.

The degree award that you will receive on successfully completing your degree will also reflect the rules of your university. For an honours degree, you will be given a classification, normally classified as First Class, Upper Second Class, Lower Second Class and Third. As part of the KIS, you can view the results for students on your programme by clicking on the 'Study information' tab at the top of the home page for your programme. There you will find a pie chart showing the proportion of First Class and other degrees awarded.

There are a few universities moving towards a *Grade Point Average* system, in which you would receive an average mark instead of (or alongside) a degree classification. Check with your university website to see if this is the case, or ask during a visit.

Independent study

The whole idea of independent study is sometimes a puzzle for students. It is perhaps the most important aspect of university study, but the least understood – not least by the media or by parents, who often seem to think that the more contact hours you receive, the better the programme that you are following.

The key thing to realise here is that university sets out to help you to think for yourself, and to develop the capacity to research and evaluate situations and arguments critically without needing to be told what to do. In a work environment, you will be asked to produce reports and undertake tasks without assistance from others. Your lecturers and tutors will raise questions for you to ponder, not just give you the answers to problems. If you see this as a key part of your education from the beginning, this will hold you in good stead.

Making the most of your time at university

An important aspect of life at university is to maintain a good balance in your lifestyle. University is an opportunity to make new friends, to mix with people from other countries and cultures and to develop your social or sporting skills. In the first flush of freedom, it may be tempting to devote much of your time to the sporting, recreational or social side, especially if you think that the first year will not count towards your final award, and therefore does not matter. This is the road to complacency, as even if the first year is a 'qualifying year', it is laying the foundation for future years of the programme, and forming habits that could be difficult to break later. So, try to keep a good balance between these different aspects of your life, and do not neglect either your studies or your social, sporting or other recreational activities.

PART IV

Using economics

11

Attributes of an economics graduate

This brief chapter will:

- describe the attributes that an economics graduate is expected to have developed by the end of their programme of study

When you have finished your degree programme and get your degree, what sorts of skills and abilities will you have developed? In particular, how will your newly found status as an *economics* graduate set you apart from graduates of other disciplines?

The QAA's subject benchmark statement for economics is a useful starting point (QAA, 2015), as it discusses this explicitly, and sets out what it expects from all economics undergraduate programmes. You can see the way in which your programme delivers these skills in the programme specification, which will specify the intended programme outcomes and subject-specific skills.

There are some generic skills that would be delivered by any undergraduate honours programme. These include skills of communication, research and inquiry together with the academic attributes of understanding, critical evaluation and the capacity to work independently and reflectively. It is also hoped that graduates would develop notions of ethics and global citizenship (an awareness that we are part of a global society, respecting human rights).

Economic modelling

As you progress through your programme, you will learn about economic modelling. This entails being able to abstract from reality, simplifying in a way that helps you to create a framework that allows you to identify the essential aspects of complex systems. For example, the introduction of a new economic policy is likely to have multiple effects, some of which will be more important to economic agents than others. By being able to cut through the complexity, you will be able to focus on what really matters.

Economic reasoning

Creating a model that describes reality is the first step. Your degree should also provide you with the ability to apply the model in analysing the implications of the processes at work. The application of economic models provides you with the ability to reason logically and coherently, seeing the sequence of steps from problem to solution. It also helps that you will be familiar with the nature of the assumptions that underpin economic models, and the way in which you can learn from varying those assumptions as a way of focusing on key aspects of a problem.

Quantitative skills

A strength of an economics education is that it provides you with skills of numeracy and quantitative awareness, in a number of dimensions.

You will have become proficient in mathematics and its applications, which in turn produces the ability to think logically and to follow an argument through to its conclusion. You will also have attained familiarity with and understanding of economic data. You will be able to evaluate the performance of the economy, and to recognise when data are being misused or misrepresented by commentators with a particular axe to grind.

IT literacy

The typical economics graduate is also IT-literate, not only in relation to standard usage of spreadsheets and word processing, but also by using specialist software used by economists, for example in econometrics. If you have access to a suite of Bloomberg terminals, you will also be familiar with the software used in city trading. These are valuable as part of the skill-set of economics graduates.

Of especial value is the ability to interpret the results of mathematical or statistical analysis, and to evaluate the results.

Separating the wood from the trees

During your studies, you will have been confronted with questions or exercises that require you to distinguish between pertinent and peripheral issues.

You may have to think about which theories are relevant to a question, or to identify which economic variables are fundamental to the question and which are peripheral. This ability to focus on the theories or variables that are of central importance is another attribute of a successful economics graduate. Having learnt to do this in the context of economics, you should be able to apply the same approach elsewhere.

Problem-solving and decision-making

All of the attributes described above come together to make the economics graduate well able to tackle problems and to take good decisions. The combination of characteristics contributes to the economist's 'way of thinking', which is seen as a key part of an economics education (especially by economists). Particularly important is the ability to recognise the constraints on decision-making that come from the social and political environment.

Communication

Graduates of all subject areas should be able to communicate effectively. For an economics graduate, it is important to be able to communicate economic ideas and to explain the operation of the economy and its performance to an audience of non-economists. Presentation skills are thus important, and should form part of your education. This relates to both written and verbal communication. The ability to explain complex ideas and quantitative issues in a clear and non-technical way will be valuable in the workplace.

If your programme includes a requirement for you to undertake a dissertation or research project, this will have added to your communication skills, as you will have had to plan, carry out and present your results in a coherent and logical fashion.

Critical thinking and evaluation

An economics education teaches you to think in a critical way, taking nothing for granted, but clearly setting out the assumptions on which an argument is based. It also nurtures the ability to be reflective and evaluative, balancing the strengths and weaknesses of an argument and coming to a considered view.

Using economic concepts

Earlier in the book, some of the key concepts that appear in economic analysis were introduced. These will all be part of the toolkit available to the economics graduate. Recognising the importance of such things as opportunity cost, incentives that influence behaviour, the importance of strategic thinking, the marginal approach and the notion of equilibrium are all potentially useful as part of a decision-making process. The role of markets and the possibility of market failure are important in any discussion of economic policy.

Of course, not all of these concepts will be important for all decisions in all contexts, so being able to know when and which to bring to bear is an important skill.

Having introduced the key attributes that you can expect to have acquired as a student of economics, the next and final chapter moves on to show which of these skills are especially valued by employers, and the variety of occupations in which those skills can be put to use.

Reference

Quality Assurance Agency (QAA) (2015) *Subject Benchmark Statement: Economics*. Part of the UK Quality Code for Higher Education. Available at http://www.qaa.ac.uk/en/Publications/Documents/SBS-Economics-15.pdf

12

Prospects for you as an economics graduate

- look at the prospects facing a graduate from an economics undergraduate degree programme
- explore the skills that employers look for when recruiting graduates
- match those skills against the attributes of a typical economics graduate
- examine some evidence on how employers perceive the value of recruiting economics graduates
- look at the possible career destinations of economics graduates
- discuss how economics can change your life

What happens when you reach the end of your programme of study and you need to face the world? The previous chapter outlined the attributes that an economics graduate can be expected to have developed, but how do these help you to tackle the realities of work and life?

What do employers want?

The wide range of careers that economics graduates enter when they complete their degrees is testament to the value that employers place on the skills that the subject instils in you. However, once you have learnt about economics and its methods, you will want some more definite evidence that this rather general statement will apply to *you*.

There has been much research in recent years to discover what skills and qualities are seen as desirable by employers wanting to recruit graduates. An important first point to notice is that from the employer perspective, it is not only the skills that are important; it is also about attitudes and personal qualities.

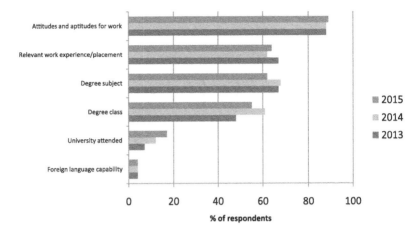

Figure 12.1 Factors considered by employers when recruiting graduates (*Source:* Based on data from CBI (2015)).

Some important work has been undertaken by the Confederation of British Industry (CBI) in this area. The CBI represents 190,000 businesses, employing more than seven million workers in the UK. Figure 12.1 shows the most important factors considered by employers when recruiting graduates. These results come from the annual surveys carried out in 2013, 2014 and 2015.

You can see that the most frequently cited factor was attitudes and aptitudes for work. This encompasses employability skills (aptitudes), but attitudes are also important. A joint report from Universities UK (UUK) and the CBI (2009) lists nine key employability skills:

- Self-management
- Teamworking
- Business and customer awareness
- Problem solving
- Communication and literacy
- Application of numeracy
- Application of information technology
- A positive attitude
- Entrepreneurship/enterprise

UUK/CBI (2009)

These are generic skills that are delivered to varying degrees by a range of different discipline-based programmes. However, if you compare the list with the economics graduate attributes outlined in Chapter 11, you will find that economics is well situated to be able to provide the sorts of broad skills that employers say that they want when they are recruiting graduates.

In an attempt to focus more closely on the specific skills of economics graduates, the *Economics Network* carries out a regular survey of employers of economics graduates. This survey aims to improve the understanding of the skills and knowledge that economics graduates need to be effective in the workplace. The 2014–15 survey was carried out with the support of the Government Economic Service and the Society of Business Economists. Figure 12.2 shows how employers viewed some of the skills seen to be attained by economics graduates.

These results look promising for when you graduate with an economics degree, as there seems to be a close match between the attributes that economics graduates are expected to attain and the qualities that employers wish to see. However, it is interesting to note that the understanding and interpretation of financial matters and the ability to formulate economic problems are less strongly regarded than some of the other attributes.

Another perspective is offered by some international evidence from Graduate Careers Australia (2014). A survey of employers was undertaken, as part of which respondents were asked whether they had experienced difficulty in recruiting graduates from certain disciplines. Of those who had, the highest discipline mentioned was Information Technology, which was mentioned by 29.2% of employers; the second highest was Business and Economics,

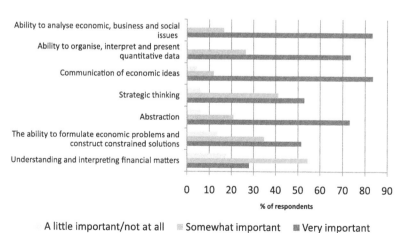

Figure 12.2 **Which skills do employers see as important for economics graduates? (*Source:* Data from *Economics Network* (2015)).**

mentioned by 26.4%. No other subject was mentioned by more than 20% of respondents. This suggests that there is some scarcity of economics graduates compared to those studying other subjects.

It is one thing to discover something of what employers look for as attributes of economics graduates. However, it is also crucial to find whether the expectations of employers are met when they recruit economics graduates. In other words, how highly do employers rate the skills and attributes that their recruits have developed? This is explored in the next section.

How do employers value the attributes of economics graduates?

At a general level, there has been some debate about the extent to which graduates from university have the requisite skills and competencies that employers are looking for in their recruits. For example, the CBI's annual survey collects views from employers about the work-relevant skills of graduates. Some results from the 2015 survey are shown in Figure 12.3, focusing on some of the skills that would be expected to be developed by graduates from an economics degree.

Remember that these results refer to *all* graduates, not just those who have studied economics, but this may be useful as a benchmark for the results more specific to economics graduates. In particular, notice that employers tend to be relatively satisfied with the IT, technical, quantitative, analysis and problem-solving skills, with 80% or more of respondents saying they are satisfied or very satisfied. Views about teamworking and communication skills are lower, but still rated as satisfactory by more than 70% of employers.

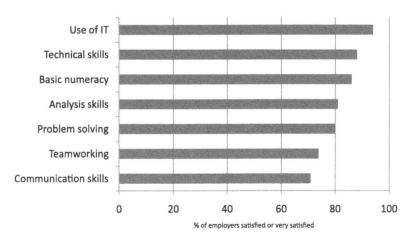

% of employers satisfied or very satisfied

Figure 12.3 Employer satisfaction with graduates' work-relevant skills (%). (*Source:* Selected data from CBI (2015)).

University league tables include a measure of graduate prospects or employability (although they do not all use the same measures). This has meant that universities have paid increasing attention to the employability of their graduates, whilst at the same time arguing that they exist to provide a high-quality education to their students, not to be a training ground focusing on skills.

Nonetheless, from your position as a potential student, this does mean that your degree will provide qualities that will be useful in the workplace, and your university will provide careers advice and support. The question is how economics compares with other disciplines in fostering the attributes that employers value. Figure 12.4 offers some evidence drawn from the *Economics Network Annual Employers' Survey*, which focuses on the skills of economics graduates.

On the basis of these data, economics graduates seem to be rated relatively more highly in the *Economics Network* survey than by the CBI. Notice that we need to be very careful in making statements about this, as the two surveys ask different questions and cover different employers. The results are therefore at best speculative or very tentative (and as an economics graduate you would be very aware of this!).

Subject to those reservations, economics graduates score very well in analysis skills and team working, as compared to the CBI more general survey, but slightly less well on IT skills (although the score is over 90%). It would also appear that economists communicate well in speech, but less well in writing.

Please be aware that these results are not conclusive, and your personal characteristics will also play a part. However, they do appear to indicate

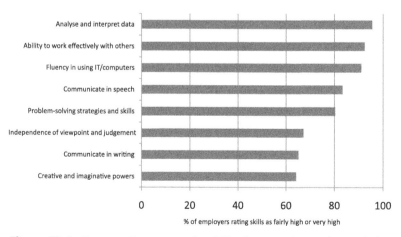

Figure 12.4 **How employers rate the skills of economics graduates (%)** (***Source:*** **Selected data from *Economics Network Employers' Survey 2014–15*).**

131

that the employability skills of economics graduates are well-regarded by employers.

The *Network*'s survey also asked about some specific areas of knowledge and understanding in economics that they saw as important. The most important for employers were incentives and their effects (94% 'very' or 'somewhat' important), opportunity cost (91%) and connections with economic phenomena (89%); the least regarded was equilibrium and disequilibrium (70%).

Career destinations

What do economics graduates do when they finish their degrees?

The main source of information about the destinations of graduates is a national survey that is carried out by the Higher Education Statistics Agency (HESA). This is the Destination of Leavers from Higher Education (DLHE) survey. In this survey all graduates from an undergraduate programme are contacted to find out what they are doing six months after graduation. Typically the survey is answered by about three-quarters of graduates, and the results are publicly available on the HESA website (https://www.hesa.ac.uk/stats-dlhe). The results also form part of the information made available as part of the KIS dataset, so you can see the destinations of past graduates on your chosen degree programme. The results for individual subjects are also provided. Figure 12.5 shows the results from 4,470 students who graduated with economics degrees in 2013, compared with graduates from all subjects.

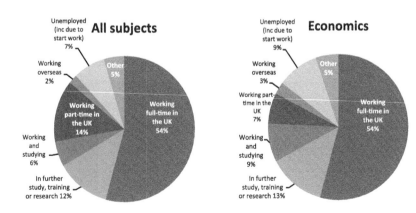

Figure 12.5 **Destination of graduates 2013 (after 6 months) (*Source:* Data from http://www.hecsu.ac.uk/current_projects_what_ do_graduates_do.htm).**

These data are based on the results of the DLHE survey. You can see that in fact the pattern for economics graduate is not very different from the average across all subjects. Again, the data should be treated with some caution, as it could be argued that undertaking a survey after only six months may be too soon to judge the long-run position.

The DLHE survey also asks respondents to report on the type of work they were doing. For some subjects, the occupational direction for graduates is clear. An obvious example would be medicine, where the vast majority of students who complete a medical degree go on to enter the medical profession.

For economics, it is not so clear, as the degree prepares you for employment in a wide range of occupations. Some economics graduates will continue to study the subject further by following a Master's degree, and some of those may go on to take a doctorate (PhD). For those who enter the workplace, some may look for a job in the public sector, and an economics degree fits you particularly well for the Government Economic Service or the Bank of England. In the private sector, there are openings for economists to look for employment in the financial or banking sector, or to get a job as a business or management professional.

To find out about the sorts of jobs taken by people who have followed your chosen programme, go to the Unistats website and the KIS for your programme. If you go to the 'Employment and accreditation' tab, you will find useful information, which includes a list of the most common jobs taken up by graduates in recent years.

Alongside this information, you will also find data on average salaries after six months and after 40 months, and data about the proportion who go on to work and/or study, and whether their employment after six months is in a professional ('graduate') job. All of these data come from the DLHE survey. Of course, you can compare the data with other programmes, which may be useful if you are still deciding about where to apply.

The Complete University Guide has compiled data from the DLHE survey about the starting salaries of graduates by subject. Economics was ranked sixth of all subjects in 2012, after dentistry, chemical engineering, medicine, general and mechanical engineering.

Starting salaries are not everything of course – what is important is the pattern of earnings across your lifetime. Walker and Zhu (2013) used data from the *Labour Force Survey* to estimate the returns to education for different major subjects studied by graduates, making use of econometric techniques. In this study, economics graduates showed the highest returns apart from medical-related subjects, coming ahead of law graduates, who were in third place.

The *Economics Network* has produced a series of videos, in which economics graduates talk about their experience in employment in a variety of occupations. This will give you a flavour of what to expect (http://whystudyeconomics. ac.uk/After-you-graduate/case-studies/)

Economics for life

Your time spent at university is partly a consumption good – a time to experience new things and to build a network of new friends. However, it is also an investment good – it prepares you for your life after university by building up your human capital.

This investment in your human capital brings a range of benefits. You will emerge from your programme with new skills and abilities related to your studies, as we have discussed. However, you will also have developed your communication and interpersonal skills, and gained the ability to be independent – in particular to be an independent and reflective learner. In other words, you will not only have learnt to *do* things, but you will have learnt how to carry out research – to find out things independently, and to pick your way around the vast amount of information that pervades the internet.

As an economics graduate, you will be in a strong position to understand the way in which government impinges on our lives through its economic policy. You will be able to understand why a particular policy would be introduced, and to anticipate the impact it will have on the behaviour of people and businesses.

You will be able to see behind the statistics presented in the media, and recognise when these are being manipulated by people wanting to impose their point of view on others. This economic literacy will give you a head start in keeping up with current affairs and in forming your own views about politics and the economy.

These life skills will be of value to you in your working life, and contribute to your success in whatever career you decide to pursue. However, the approach that characterises the economist will also add value to your life outside the workplace. Notions of opportunity cost, cost–benefit analysis, the margin or sunk costs will become part of the way in which you think about problems and approach decision-making. This may not always be a conscious part of your life, but once you are an economist, it will colour your thinking process.

The decision-making and problem-solving skills that you develop in an economics degree can be applied in the decisions that you take, and the problems that you may face. This applies to the little decisions that you take every day of your life, but also to the big decisions that shape your life-course. Using the economic approach to decisions and problems provides a coherent and logical framework for analysing situations and reaching good decisions, although there will undoubtedly be times when your heart may come to rule your brain, and rightly so.

I found economics to be a challenging but fascinating subject to study, and if you choose to study it I believe you will find the same. It will change the way you view the world, and will open doors into new experiences. The world is changing rapidly, and graduates today need to be flexible: ready to understand and embrace change in the workplace and in living. In the future you may find yourself in jobs or careers that do not even exist yet. Economics provides a sound foundation for dealing with risk and uncertainty and for adapting to unfamiliar situations. By learning to think like an economist, you can be ready for anything. Enjoy your studies, and make the most of your life.

References

CBI (2013) *Changing the Pace: CBI/Pearson Education and Skill Survey 2013*. London: Pearson. Available at http://www.cbi.org.uk/media/2119176/education_and_skills_survey_2013.pdf

CBI (2014) *Gateway to Growth: CBI/Pearson Education and Skills Survey 2014*. London: Pearson. Available at http://www.cbi.org.uk/media/2807987/gateway-to-growth.pdf

CBI (2015) *Inspiring Growth: CBI/Pearson Education and Skills Survey 2015*. London: Pearson. Available at http://news.cbi.org.uk/reports/education-and-skills-survey-2015/education-and-skills-survey-2015/

Economics Network. *Employers' Survey 2014-15*. Available at http://www.economics network.ac.uk/projects/surveys/employers14-15

Graduate Careers Australia (2014) *Graduate Outlook 2013*. Melbourne: Graduate Opportunities. Available at http://www.graduateopportunities.com/your-career/getting-that-job/what-employers-want/

UUK/CBI (2009) *Future Fit: Preparing Graduates for the World of Work*. Available at http://www.i-graduate.org/assets/2011-Employability-Report-published-by-BIS.pdf

Walker, I. and Zhu, Y. (2013) *The Impact of University Degrees on the Lifecycle of Earnings: Some Further Analysis*. London: Department of Business, Innovation and Skills. Available at https://www.gov.uk/government/uploads/system/uploads/attachment_data/file/229498/bis-13-899-the-impact-of-university-degrees-on-the-lifecycle-of-earnings-further-analysis.pdf

Useful questions to ask at an open (visit) day

When you reach the stage of choosing which university you want to attend, it is important to make the most of invitations to visit those on your shortlist. Such invitations may happen when you have applied or when you are offered a conditional place. There may be opportunities to visit on a general open day that universities arrange.

On these organised visits, you will meet staff who are involved in the admissions process and you will have the opportunity to talk with lecturers and current students. These are all people who can offer you invaluable information to help guide your choices. Make the most of it, and if for some reason you cannot attend on the day, see whether you can visit at another time. Failing that, make good use of the university website. They may have a virtual tour that you can watch online, but this should be seen as the last resort if you cannot attend a visit; it is not a substitute for being there.

One way of making sure that you make the best of your visit is to go prepared. Study the prospectus and the website before you go, and familiarise yourself with key information about the university. There is no point in arriving to ask questions about information that is readily available on the website, such as normal entry requirements.

Here are some questions that you might want to ask while you are on campus. Of course, this is not exhaustive, but they may give you ideas about the issues that you will be especially interested to explore.

You are likely to meet administrative staff involved in the admissions process, and admissions tutors who are members of the academic staff. I have divided the questions between these three groups, but do not regard them as being too separate. You may wish to ask the same question to academic staff and to students (to see if you get the same answer!), or you may find that administrative staff refer you on to the lecturers, or vice versa. Nonetheless, in general it makes sense to ask questions to whoever is best placed to provide an answer.

Questions to staff involved in admissions

Questions for this group should focus on their area of expertise: on the mechanics of the admissions process, or on the facilities available.

- Are there scholarship or bursaries available for students?
- How likely is it that there will be flexibility in relation to entry requirements at clearing and confirmation if I marginally miss my required grades?
- Do you count Maths and Further Maths as one A-level or two?
- Do you view applicants without Economics differently from those who have studied the subject?
- How does the university regard EPQ?
- What are the entry requirements for BTEC/IB/etc.?
- Is it possible to transfer between programmes

    - before I arrive
    - on arrival
    - at a later stage (e.g. at the end of the first year?

- Are there opportunities for placements, work experience or internships during the programme?
- Are there opportunities to spend time on a study abroad programme?

    - If so, where?
    - Are there opportunities to study abroad where the teaching is in English?

- Is it possible to get evening or part-time work near or on the campus?
- What induction arrangements will there be at the beginning of the programme?
- What computing and IT facilities are available?
- What guidance will be available in terms of careers?
- Will there be an opportunity to meet with former students at any point?
- What student societies are there that are especially helpful for economics students?
- Please may I have a copy of your slides from the presentation?

Questions to academic staff

- Is there flexibility in the curriculum?

    - What is the range of options available, including specialist options?
    - Are there possibilities for combining with another subject?

- Do you offer major/minor combinations?
- Will I be able to take options from outside of economics as part of my programme?

• Are there opportunities for undertaking a research project or dissertation?
• Please tell me about how I will be assessed.

- To what extent does the assessment rely on unseen written examinations?

• How varied are the styles of learning and teaching?
• How large are the lecture groups?
• How large are the class/seminar groups?
• How much prior knowledge is expected in relation to mathematics and/or economics?
• Is there any preparation I should do before arriving (e.g. reading)?
• Are students without A-level Economics taught separately in year 1?
• Are students without A-level Mathematics taught separately in year 1?
• How much contact will I have with my personal tutor?
• What are the distinctive features of your programme?
• What sorts of jobs do your graduates obtain?
• Are there possibilities for further study in economics at postgraduate level when I finish my degree?
• Do you have a suite of Bloomberg terminals?
• Is there an experimental lab for economics?

- Could I take part in experiments?

• Does your department participate in the CORE project?

Questions to current students

There are several questions above which you could also address to students, in particular in relation to assessment and feedback, styles of learning and teaching, contact with your tutors and lecturers etc.

• What do you like best about your programme?
• What do you like least about your programme?
• How approachable and accessible are the academic staff?
• What clubs and societies do you recommend for economics students?

- or for any students?

• How comfortable are the university residencies?
• What is the availability of private accommodation within reach of the campus?

- Is this in good areas?

- What are the social facilities like?

    - on and off campus?

- How good are the transport links in the city?
- How good are the student support services?
- Please tell me about the assessment methods, feedback provided and the workload needed.
- How good are the facilities for students, such as computing, library and other academic support?
- Do you feel secure in the university and its surrounds?
- How easy is it to meet people and to form networks?

After the visit

Take notes of your visit, otherwise you will forget things, especially if you are visiting several different universities.

As part of your note-taking, reflect on key things that may affect your decision, such as

- location
- environment
- ambiance
- friendliness of the students
- approachability of the lecturers and administrative staff
- facilities

    - study
    - social

- programme content

Glossary of key terms and concepts

Absolute advantage: a situation in which a country can produce a good more efficiently than another, for example requiring less labour

Aggregate demand: the total level of demand for goods and services in an economy

Aggregate supply: the total level goods and services supplied by firms in an economy

Allocative efficiency: a situation in which firms collectively are producing an appropriate mix of goods and services that people in an economy wish to consume

Asymmetric information: a situation in which some parties to a transaction have better information than others

Balance of payments: a set of accounts summarising the transactions between residents of a country and the rest of the world

Bank rate: the interest rate set by the Bank of England to influence other interest rates set by financial institutions

Barter: a system in which transactions are carried out without money

Benefit–cost analysis: a technique in which the benefits of an activity (in particular a large-scale project) are balanced against its costs, taking into account externalities, and calculating the present value of future costs by discounting the future; it is sometimes known as cost–benefit analysis

Capital: machinery, buildings, transport equipment and other produced resources used as inputs into the production process: an important factor of production

Comparative advantage: a situation in which a country has a relative efficiency advantage in the production of a product compared with another country, even if it does not have an absolute advantage

Competition and Markets Authority (CMA): the body in the UK responsible for implementing competition policy, promoting competition and protecting consumer interests

Competition policy: measures taken by government to promote competition in the economy

Consumption (C): total spending on goods and services by households; an important component of aggregate demand

Current account of the balance of payments: the section of the balance of payments accounts that records transactions in goods and services between the residents of a country and the rest of the world

Deflation: a situation in which the overall price level in an economy is falling

Demand curve: a curve that shows the quantity demanded of a good at any given price

Division of labour: a form of specialisation identified by Adam Smith, in which the efficiency of production can be improved by having workers specialise in certain parts of the production process

Dollar standard: a system under which exchange rates were pegged to the US$; this operated in the post-war period, but broke down in the early 1970s

Duopoly: a market in which there are two sellers of a good or service

Econometrics: the application of mathematical and statistical techniques to economic data in order to test economic hypotheses and theories

Economic agents: entities that take economic decisions; households or individuals, firms and governments

Economic growth: the rate at which overall economic activity in an economy grows from one period to the next, often measured by the rate of change of GDP or GNI

Elasticity: a measure of the sensitivity of one economic variable to a change in some other variable

Equilibrium: a state of balance between opposing forces, for example, between demand and supply in a market

Exports (X): spending by residents of an economy on goods or services produced in the domestic economy by the rest of the world

Externality: a cost or benefit in a market that is borne by a third party, and not reflected in the market price of a good or service

Factors of production: inputs used in the production process, such as labour, land and capital

Financial crisis: a situation that arose in the late 2000s, in which a number of banks were in danger of failing; the crisis had significant repercussions for the real economy

Fiscal policy: part of macroeconomic policy in which the government uses its spending and taxation to influence the economy

Free-rider problem: arises from the nature of public goods, where individual consumers cannot be excluded from consuming a good or service once it is provided

Full employment: a situation in which labour is fully utilised, although this does not necessarily mean there is no unemployment, as workers may be between jobs

Game theory: an approach to the study of strategic interaction (for example, between firms) that helps to analyse conflict and co-operation

General Agreement on Tariffs and Trade (GATT): an institution set up to oversee the dollar standard and to encourage reductions in tariff levels; set up at the Bretton Woods conference in 1944 but replaced in 1995 by the World Trade Organisation

Government expenditure (G): spending by government on goods and services; a component of aggregate demand

Gross domestic product (GDP): the total amount of economic activity in a the domestic economy during a period of time

Gross national income (GNI): GDP plus net income from abroad

Human capital: the stock of skills, expertise and physical qualities that contribute to a worker's productivity

Imports (M): spending on domestically produced goods and services by the rest of the world

Inflation: the rate of change of the overall price level in an economy

International Monetary Fund (IMF): a multilateral institution that was set up at the 1944 Bretton Woods conference to provide short-term financing for countries experiencing severe imbalances in their balance of payments

Interest rate: the rate that is charged to borrowers on loans from financial institutions

Investment (I): expenditure by firms to maintain and expand their stock of capital; a component of aggregate demand

Invisible hand: the name given by Adam Smith to the process by which price signals guide the allocation of resources in a society

Labour: the factor of production supplied by workers

Law of diminishing marginal returns: a law that states that increasing the input of one factor of production whilst maintaining the level of input of other factors will eventually cause the additional output produced by an extra unit of the variable factor to fall

Macroeconomics: the study of the relationships between economic variables at the aggregate (economy) level

Marginal analysis: the notion that economic agents may take decisions by considering marginal (small) changes from a current position

Marginal propensity to consume: the proportion of additional income spent on consumption

Market: a set of arrangements that allow transactions to take place between buyers and sellers of a good or service

Market failure: a situation in which a free market fails to produce the best outcome for society

Microeconomics: the study of economic behaviour of individual economic agents

Millennium Development Goals (MDGs): a set of eight targets agreed at the UN Millennium Summit in 2000 to reduce extreme poverty

Monetary policy: the use of interest rates or money supply to influence the level of aggregate demand in the economy

Money supply: the total stock of money in an economy at any point in time

Multiplier: a process described by Keynes whereby an initial amount of autonomous spending has multiplied effects on aggregate demand

Monopoly: a market in which there is one seller

Nationalisation: where a private firm or industry is taken into public ownership

Neoclassical economics: an approach to economic analysis in which economic agents are assumed to act rationally and markets find equilibrium through the operation of the free market

Normative statement: a statement involving a value judgement (an expression of opinion)

Oligopoly: a market in which there are only a few sellers of a good or service

Opportunity cost: when choosing amongst alternatives, this is the value of the next best alternative choice that is sacrificed

Pareto optimality (or **Pareto efficiency):** an allocation of resource such that no reallocation could make any individual better off without making some other individual worse off

Political business cycle: where the government stimulates the economy before an election to gain popularity, only to slow the economy down afterwards

Positive statement: a statement based on objective analysis that does not involve a value judgement

Price elasticity of demand: a measure of the extent to which the quantity demanded of a good or service changes in response to a change in its price, other things being equal

Principal–agent problem: a situation in which economic agents acting on behalf of their principals have better information and limited accountability: for example where the managers (agents) of a firm are not fully accountable to the shareholders (principals), and can thus pursue their own interests

Privatisation: where a publicly owned firm or industry is transferred into private ownership

Productive efficiency: a situation in which a firm is minimising the cost of producing a given level of output of a good or service

Productivity: a measure of the efficiency of a factor of production: for example labour productivity is the output produced per unit of labour

Profit: the return that a firm receives from its economic activities: the excess of revenue over cost

Quantitative easing: a measure introduced by the Bank of England in the aftermath of the financial crisis of the late 2000s to increase the flow of credit in the economy

Scarcity: the notion that all individuals and societies face a situation of limited resources relative to their unlimited wants

Structure–conduct–performance paradigm: the idea that the performance of a market in terms of resource allocation would be determined by the conduct of the firms in the market, which in turn would be determined by the structure of the market

Supply curve: a curve that shows the quantity supplied by firms of a good at any given price

Supply-side policies: measures introduced to have a direct effect on aggregate supply

Sustainable development: 'development which meets the needs of the present without compromising the ability of future generations to meet their own needs' (Brundtland Commission, 1987)

Sustainable Development Goals: a set of targets adopted after the deadline for the Millennium Development Goals had passed

Threshold concepts: a series of fundamental ideas that underpin economic analysis

Unemployment rate: the percentage of the workforce looking for work and able to work who are unable to find a job

Utility: the satisfaction that an individual gains from an economic action – for example, from consuming a good or service

Washington Consensus: a set of standard policies characterising the approach to encouraging development in less-developed countries by such organisations as the IMF and the World Bank

World Bank: a multilateral organisation that provides funding for long-term development projects in less-developed countries

World Trade Organisation (WTO): a multilateral body responsible for overseeing the conduct of international trade, including dispute settlement

Additional resources

There is a wealth of resources available on the internet that will help to guide you in your decisions about whether and where to study economics at university. For each Part, some advice is provided below on how to locate these and how to use them effectively.

There are also some key organisations whose websites will be helpful more generally.

For anyone applying for a UK undergraduate degree programme, a key organisation is UCAS, as all applications must pass through them. Their website is at https://www.ucas.com/

The Unistats website at https://unistats.direct.gov.uk/ is another key place to start, and is a link into the Key Information Sets that universities are required to provide about each of their undergraduate programmes. References to this site are provided in various parts of the book where this is relevant.

The Quality Assurance Agency is the regulatory body for universities in the UK, and provides benchmark statements for the main subjects that are studied in degree programmes that set out what is expected to be delivered by any degree programme. The national subject benchmark for economics was revised in 2015 and can be found at http://www.qaa.ac.uk/en/Publications/Documents/SBS-Economics-15.pdf

The A-level Examination Boards provide information about the content of their A-level Economics programmes, and provide links to teaching materials and textbooks. Their websites are at the following locations.

AQA

http://www.aqa.org.uk/

Information about the Economics A-level is at
http://www.aqa.org.uk/subjects/economics

Edexcel

http://qualifications.pearson.com/en/home.html

The Economics A page is at
http://qualifications.pearson.com/en/qualifications/edexcel-a-levels/
    economics-a-2015.html#tab-Teaching

OCR

http://www.ocr.org.uk/

Information about the A-level Economics programme is at
http://www.ocr.org.uk/qualifications/as-a-level-gce-economics-h060-h460-
    from-2015/

For Northern Ireland, see
http://ccea.org.uk/economics/

For Wales, see
http://www.wjec.co.uk/qualifications/economics/

Another very useful site that provides advice and guidance about economics is the *Economics Network* site. The *Economics Network* was formerly the national subject centre for economics that operated under the aegis of the Higher Education Academy, but which now is an independent body based at the University of Bristol funded by sponsors and by subscriptions from university departments of economics. The website can be found at http://www.economicsnetwork.ac.uk/

Of particular interest to you will be the 'Why Study Economics' page at http://whystudyeconomics.ac.uk/

The book draws on material from the *Economics Network* at various points.

In general, I would not recommend you to start finding out about economics by reading textbooks in the subject, although you will find references to some AS- and A-level textbooks through the Exam Board websites above.

However, you might like to visit the Sloman Economics news site at http://pearsonblog.campaignserver.co.uk/?page_id=507

This provides up-to-date blogs about economic issues, which you may find to be interesting and will give you a flavour of how economic analysis can be brought to bear on topics of current interest.

Part I: Defining economics

Economics is a subject that can be applied to questions that arise in a variety of situations. To get a feel for this without needing to know much about economics, there are several recent books that are written in a style that will get you thinking like an economist. They will also demonstrate some of the challenges of the subject and the potential fascination that many people find in the subject. Examples are the following:

Chang, H-J. (2014) *Economics: The User's Guide*. Bloomsbury Press.

Harford, T. (2005) *The Undercover Economist*. Oxford University Press.

Harford, T. (2014) *The Undercover Economist Strikes Back*. New York: Penguin.

Levitt, S.D. and Dubner, S.J. (2005) *Freakonomics*. New York: Harper Collins.

Levitt, S.D. and Dubner, S.J. (2009) *Superfreakonomics*. New York: Harper Collins.

Levitt, S.D. and Dubner, S.J. (2014) *Think Like a Freak: The Authors of Freakonomics Offer to Retrain your Brain*. New York: Harper Collins.

Pryce, V., Ross, A. and Unwin, P. (2015) *It's the Economy, Stupid: Economics for Voters*. Biteback.

In looking at the origins of economic thinking, many of the original texts are somewhat inaccessible to the modern reader, but I have cited the original texts below for completeness. If you want to find out more, you could consult one of the many books on the history of economic thought, such as:

Backhouse, R.E. (2002) *The Penguin History of Economics*. Penguin: London.

Part II: The scope of economics

To find out more about the work of the Competition and Markets Authority and how they try to promote competition and protect consumers, visit their website at https://www.gov.uk/government/organisations/competition-and-markets-authority

To find out about the Millennium Sustainable Development Goals, visit http://www.un.org/sustainabledevelopment/sustainable-development-goals/

To read more about the winners of the Nobel Memorial Prize for Economic Sciences, go to http://www.nobelprize.org/nobel_prizes/economic-sciences/laureates/

Part III: Studying economics

The *Economics Network* website offers some useful guidance on how to study economics:

http://www.economicsnetwork.ac.uk/

The University of Wolverhampton has provided a useful interactive map showing the location of higher education institutions in the UK. You can find this at http://www.scit.wlv.ac.uk/ukinfo/index.php

An important website to help you to find your preferred degree programme is the Unistats site at https://unistats.direct.gov.uk/find-out-more/key-information-set

The QAA economics subject benchmarks are found at http://www.qaa.ac.uk/en/Publications/Documents/SBS-Economics-15.pdf

Information about the CORE project can be found at http://www.core-econ.org/ (Free registration is needed if you want to access the ebook.)

If you want to browse some economic data about countries around the world, try the World Bank's Data Visualizer at http://devdata.worldbank.org/DataVisualizer/

Data produced by the United Nations Development Programme can be viewed at http://hdr.undp.org/en/data

The SDGs (Global Goals) are set out at http://www.undp.org/content/undp/en/home/mdgoverview/post-2015-development-agenda.html

Part IV: Using economics

Again, visit the QAA benchmark document cited above to find out more about the attributes expected to be achieved by an economics graduate.

The *Economics Network* website also offers helpful information. For example, you may wish to look at http://whystudyeconomics.ac.uk/After-you-graduate/case-studies/

A useful general website for graduates, whether they want to find a job or a postgraduate course of study, is at http://www.prospects.ac.uk/

Index

For Product Safety Concerns and Information please contact our EU representative GPSR@taylorandfrancis.com Taylor & Francis Verlag GmbH, Kaufingerstraße 24, 80331 München, Germany

Printed and bound by CPI Group (UK) Ltd, Croydon, CR0 4YY
08/05/2025
01864381-0001